## U.S.NRC
United States Nuclear Regulatory Commission

*Protecting People and the Environment*

NUREG-0847
Supplement 25

I0413213

# Safety Evaluation Report

Related to the Operation of
Watts Bar Nuclear Plant, Unit 2

Docket Number 50-391

**Tennessee Valley Authority**

Office of Nuclear Reactor Regulation

# AVAILABILITY OF REFERENCE MATERIALS
# IN NRC PUBLICATIONS

United States Nuclear Regulatory Commission

*Protecting People and the Environment*

NUREG-0847
Supplement 25

# Safety Evaluation Report

## Related to the Operation of Watts Bar Nuclear Plant, Unit 2

## Docket Number 50-391

### Tennessee Valley Authority

Manuscript Completed: November 2011
Date Published: December 2011

Office of Nuclear Reactor Regulation

# ABSTRACT

This report supplements the safety evaluation report (SER), NUREG-0847 (June 1982), Supplement No. 24 (September 2011, Agencywide Documents Access and Management System (ADAMS) Accession No. ML11277A148), with respect to the application filed by the Tennessee Valley Authority (TVA), as applicant and owner, for a license to operate Watts Bar Nuclear Plant (WBN) Unit 2 (Docket No 50-391).

In its SER and Supplemental SER (SSER) Nos. 1 through 20 issued by the Office of Nuclear Reactor Regulation (NRR) of the U.S. Nuclear Regulatory Commission (NRC or the staff), the staff documented its safety evaluation and determination that WBN Unit 1 met all applicable regulations and regulatory guidance. Based on satisfactory findings from all applicable inspections, on February 7, 1996, the NRC issued a full-power operating license (OL) to WBN Unit 1, authorizing operation up to 100-percent power.

In SSER 21, the staff addressed TVA's application for a license to operate WBN Unit 2, and provided information regarding the status of the items remaining to be resolved, which were outstanding at the time that TVA deferred construction of WBN Unit 2, and were not evaluated and resolved as part of the licensing of WBN Unit 1. Beginning with SSER 22, the staff documented its ongoing evaluation and closure of open items in support of TVA's application for a license to operate WBN Unit 2.

In this and future SSERs, the staff continues its documentation of its review of open items in support of TVA's application for an operating license for WBN Unit 2.

# TABLE OF CONTENTS

## TABLE OF CONTENTS (Continued)

# ABBREVIATIONS

| | |
|---|---|
| ABGTS | auxiliary building gas treatment system |
| AC or ac | alternating current |
| ADAMS | Agencywide Documents Access and Management System |
| ALARA | as low as reasonably achievable |
| ANSI | American National Standards Institute |
| ANS | American Nuclear Society |
| ASME | American Society of Mechanical Engineers |
| AST | alternative source term |
| ASTM | American Society for Testing and Materials |
| BEACON | Westinghouse Best Estimate Analyzer for Core Operations—Nuclear |
| BL | bulletin |
| BTP | Branch Technical Position |
| BWR | boiling-water reactor |
| CAP | corrective action program |
| CCS | component cooling system |
| CET | core exit thermocouple |
| cfm | cubic feet per minute |
| CFR | Code of Federal Regulations |
| CI | confirmatory issue |
| Ci | curie |
| CLB | current licensing basis |
| COMS | cold overpressure mitigation system |
| COT | channel operability test |
| CR | control room |
| CSST | common station service transformer |
| CST | condensate storage tank |
| $C_v$ | Charpy V-notch |
| DBA | design basis accident |
| DC or dc | direct current |
| DCF | dose conversion factor |
| DCN | design change notice |
| DCS | distributed control system |
| DEI | dose equivalent iodine-131 |
| DF | decontamination factor |
| D/Q | deposition factor |
| EAB | exclusion area boundary |
| ECCS | emergency core cooling system |
| EDCR | Engineering Document Construction Release |
| EDG | emergency diesel generator |
| EGTS | emergency gas treatment system |
| EMC | electromagnetic compatibility |
| EMI/RFI | electromagnetic/radiofrequency interference |
| EOF | emergency operations facility |
| EOP | emergency operating procedure |
| EPA | Environmental Protection Agency or electrical penetration assemblies |

| | |
|---|---|
| EPRI | Electric Power Research Institute |
| EQ | environmental qualification |
| ERCW | essential raw cooling water |
| ERDS | emergency response data system |
| ESF | engineered safety feature |
| FHA | fuel handling accident |
| FSAR | final safety analysis report |
| FW | feedwater |
| GDC | general design criterion/criteria |
| GL | generic letter |
| gpm | gallons per minute |
| GSI | generic safety issue |
| HEPA | high efficiency particulate air |
| HRCAR | high range containment air radiation |
| HVAC | heating, ventilation, and air conditioning |
| ICC | inadequate core cooling |
| ICRP | International Commission on Radiological Protection |
| ICS | integrated computer system |
| IE | Office of Inspection and Enforcement |
| IEB | Office of Inspection and Enforcement Bulletin |
| IEEE | Institute of Electrical and Electronics Engineers |
| IIS | in-core instrumentation system |
| IITA | in-core instrumentation thimble assembly |
| IPE | individual plant examination |
| IPEEE | individual plant examination of external events |
| JFD | joint frequency distribution |
| kHz | kilohertz |
| kV | kilovolt |
| kVA | kilovolt ampere |
| kW | kilowatt |
| LOCA | loss-of-coolant accident |
| LOOP | loss of offsite power |
| LPMS | loose part monitoring system |
| LPZ | low-population zone |
| LTOP | low-temperature overpressure protection |
| LWR | light-water reactor |
| MSIV | main steam isolation valve |
| MSLB | main steam line break |
| MTEB | Materials Engineering Branch (of NRR) |
| MTP | maintenance and test panel |
| MVA | megavolt-ampere |
| MWt | megawatts thermal |
| NGDC | New Generation Development and Construction |
| NPP | Nuclear Performance Plan |
| NP-REP | Nuclear Power Radiological Emergency Plan |
| NRC | Nuclear Regulatory Commission |

| | |
|---|---|
| NRR | Office of Nuclear Reactor Regulation |
| NSSS | nuclear steam supply system |
| NUREG | report prepared by NRC staff |
| OBE | operating basis earthquake |
| ODCM | Offsite Dose Calculation Manual |
| OL | operating license |
| OSG | original steam generator |
| PAD | performance analysis and design |
| PAMS | postaccident monitoring system |
| PDR | public document room |
| PMF | probable maximum flood |
| PORV | power-operated relief valve |
| PTLR | Pressure and Temperature Limits Report |
| PWR | pressurized-water reactor |
| RAI | request for additional information |
| RBPVS | reactor building purge ventilation system |
| RCCA | rod cluster control assembly |
| RCS | reactor coolant system |
| RG | Regulatory Guide |
| RPM | revolutions per minute |
| RPV | reactor pressure vessel |
| RV | reactor vessel |
| SDD | software design description |
| SE | safety evaluation |
| SER | safety evaluation report, NUREG-0847, dated June 1982 |
| SFP | spent fuel pool |
| SG | steam generator |
| SPM | software program manual |
| SPND | self-powered neutron detector |
| SP | special program |
| SPS | signal processing system |
| SRO | senior reactor operator |
| SRP | Standard Review Plan, NUREG-0800 |
| SRS | software requirements specification |
| SSE | safe shutdown earthquake |
| SSER | Supplemental SER |
| Std. | Standard |
| SV | safety valve |
| TID | total integrated dose |
| TMI | Three Mile Island |
| TPBAR | tritium production burnable absorber rod |
| TS | technical specification |
| TSTF | Technical Specification Task Force |
| TVA | Tennessee Valley Authority |
| UHS | ultimate heat sink |
| V&V | verification and validation |
| WBA | Web-based ADAMS |
| WBN | Watts Bar Nuclear Plant |

| | |
|---|---|
| WCAP | Westinghouse Commercial Atomic Power (report) |
| WEC | Westinghouse Electric Corporation |
| WINCISE | Westinghouse INCore Information, Surveillance, and Engineering system |
| $\chi/Q$ | atmospheric dispersion estimate |

# LIST OF TABLES

# 1    INTRODUCTION AND DISCUSSION

## 1.1    Introduction

The Watts Bar Nuclear Plant (WBN or Watts Bar) is owned by the Tennessee Valley Authority (TVA) and is located in southeastern Tennessee approximately 50 miles northeast of Chattanooga. The facility consists of two Westinghouse-designed four-loop pressurized-water reactors (PWRs) within ice condenser containments.

In June 1982, the Nuclear Regulatory Commission staff (NRC staff or staff) issued safety evaluation report (SER), NUREG-0847, "Safety Evaluation Report related to the operation of Watts Bar Nuclear Plant Units 1 and 2," regarding TVA's application for licenses to operate WBN Units 1 and 2. In SER Supplements (SSERs) 1 through 20, the NRC staff concluded that WBN Unit 1 met all applicable regulations and regulatory guidance and on February 7, 1996, the NRC issued an operating license (OL) to Unit 1. TVA did not complete WBN Unit 2, and the NRC did not make conclusions regarding it.

On March 4, 2009, TVA submitted an updated application in support of its request for an OL for WBN Unit 2, pursuant to Title 10 of the *Code of Federal Regulations* (10 CFR), Part 50, "Domestic Licensing of Production and Utilization Facilities."

In SSER 21, the staff provided information regarding the status of the WBN Unit 2 items that remain to be resolved, which were outstanding at the time that TVA deferred construction of Unit 2, and which were not evaluated and resolved as part of the licensing of WBN Unit 1. In SSER 22, the staff began the documentation of its evaluation and closure of open items in support of TVA's application for a license to operate WBN Unit 2.

In this and future SSERs, the staff will continue the documentation of its evaluation and closure of open items in support of TVA's application.

The format of this document is consistent with the format and scope outlined in the "Standard Review Plan for the Review of Safety Analysis Reports for Nuclear Power Plants: LWR [Light-Water Reactor] Edition (NUREG-0800)," dated July 1981 (SRP, NUREG-0800). The staff added additional chapters to address the overall assessment of the facility, Nuclear Performance Plan issues, and other generic regulatory topics.

Each of the sections and appendices of this supplement is numbered the same as the SER section that is being updated, and the discussions are supplementary to, and not in lieu of, the discussion in the SER, unless otherwise noted. For example, Appendix E continues to list the principal contributors to the SSER. However, the chronology of the safety review correspondence previously provided in Appendix A has been discontinued, and a reference is provided instead to the NRC's Agencywide Documents Access and Management System (ADAMS) or the Public Document Room (PDR). Public correspondence exchanged between the NRC and TVA is available through ADAMS or the PDR. References listed as "not publicly available" in the SSER contain proprietary information and have been withheld from public disclosure in accordance with 10 CFR 2.390.

Appendix HH includes an Action Items Table. This table provides a status of all the open items, confirmatory issues, and proposed license conditions that must be resolved prior to completion of an NRC finding of reasonable assurance on the OL application for WBN Unit 2. The staff will maintain the Action Items Table and revise Appendix HH in future SSERs, and add new appendices, as necessary.

The NRC's ADAMS is the agency's official recordkeeping system. ADAMS has the full text of regulatory and technical documents and reports written by NRC, NRC contractors, or NRC licensees. Documents include NRC regulatory guides, NUREG-series reports, correspondence, inspection reports, and others, are assigned accession numbers. They are searchable and accessible from ADAMS. Documents are released periodically during the day in the ADAMS PUBLIC/Legacy Interface Combined (ADAMS PUBLIC) and Web-based ADAMS (WBA) interfaces; they are released once a day in Web-based Publicly Available Records System (PARS). These documents in full text can be searched using ADAMS accession numbers or specific fields and parameters such as docket number and documents dates.

More information regarding ADAMS and help for accessing documents may be obtained on the NRC Public Web site at http://www.nrc.gov/reading-rm/adams/faq.html#1.

All WBN documents may be accessed using WBN docket numbers 05000390 and 05000391 for Units 1 and 2, respectively.

The WBN Unit 2 Project Manager is Patrick D. Milano, who may be contacted by calling (301) 415-1457, by e-mail to Patrick.Milano@nrc.gov, or by writing to the following address:

> Mr. Patrick D. Milano
> U.S. Nuclear Regulatory Commission
> Mail Stop O-8H4
> Washington, D.C. 20555

## 1.2    General Plant Description

A general description of WBN Unit 2 was provided by the NRC staff in Section 1.2 of the SER (NUREG-0847, dated June 1982). TVA provided a more detailed description of WBN Unit 2 in Section 1.2, "General Plant Description," of Amendment 104 of the Final Safety Analysis Report (FSAR), dated June 3, 2011. An updated general description is provided below in this section of the SSER.

WBN Unit 2 is very similar in design to WBN Unit 1 and Sequoyah Nuclear Plant Units 1 and 2. WBN Unit 2 uses a nuclear steam supply system (NSSS) incorporating a PWR and a 4-loop reactor coolant system (RCS). The Unit 2 reactor core design rating is 3,411 megawatts thermal (MWt). The license application NSSS power level is 3,425 MWt, which includes 14 MWt from the reactor coolant pumps. The reactor core is composed of fuel rods made of slightly enriched uranium dioxide pellets enclosed in ZIRLO® tubes that are grouped and supported into assemblies. The mechanical control rods consist of rod cluster control assemblies (RCCAs) and burnable absorber rods that are inserted into the guide thimbles of the fuel assemblies. The absorber sections of the RCCAs are fabricated of silver-indium-cadmium alloy slugs sealed in stainless steel tubes. The absorber material in the burnable absorber rods is in the form of borosilicate glass sealed in stainless steel tubes. The core fuel is loaded in three regions, each using fuel of a different enrichment of uranium-235. The new fuel is introduced into the outer region, moved inward at successive refuelings, and removed from the inner region to the spent fuel pool (SFP).

Water will serve as both the moderator and the coolant. It will be circulated through the reactor vessel and core by four vertical, single-stage centrifugal pumps, one located in the cold leg of each loop. The coolant water heated by the reactor will be circulated through the four steam generators where heat will be transferred to the secondary system to produce saturated steam, and then it will be returned to the pumps to repeat the cycle. An electrically heated pressurizer connected to the hot-leg piping of one of the loops will establish and maintain the reactor coolant pressure and provide a surge chamber and a water reserve to accommodate reactor coolant volume changes during operation.

The steam produced in the steam generators will be used to drive a tandem arrangement of one double-flow high-pressure turbine and three double-flow low-pressure turbines driving a direct-coupled generator at 1800 revolutions per minute (RPM). The generator has a nameplate rating of 1,411,000 kilovolt-amperes (kVA) at 0.9 power factor with 75 pounds per square inch (psi) hydrogen pressure. The unit uses a single pass surface condenser of a horizontal, triple pressure, single shell type. Return to the steam generator is through three stages of feedwater pumping and seven stages of feedwater heating. Safety relief valves and power operated relief valves, as well as a turbine bypass to the condenser are provided in the steam lines. Cooling water from the cooling tower basin will be pumped through the tubes of the condenser to remove the heat from, and thus condense, the steam after it has passed through the main turbine. The condenser condensate then will be pumped back to the steam generator to be heated for another cycle. The condenser cooling water will be passed through two natural draft cooling towers and returned to the cooling tower basin.

The reactor will be controlled by a coordinated combination of a soluble neutron absorber (boric acid) and mechanical control rods whose drive shafts will allow the plant to accept step load changes of 10 percent and ramp load changes of 5 percent per minute over the range of 15 to 100 percent of full power under normal operating conditions. With steam bypass, the plant will also have the capability to accept a 50-percent step load rejection without reactor trip.

Plant protection systems are provided that automatically initiate appropriate action whenever a monitored condition approaches preestablished limits. These protection systems will act to shut down the reactor, close isolation valves, and initiate operation of the engineered safety features should any or all of these actions be required. Supervision and control of both the NSSS and the steam and power conversion system will be accomplished from the main control room.

The emergency core cooling system for the plant consists of accumulators, upper head injection, and both high- and low-pressure injection subsystems with provisions for recirculation of the borated water after the end of the injection phase. Various combinations of these features will ensure core cooling for the complete range of postulated coolant pipe break sizes.

The NSSS is housed in a separate free-standing steel containment structure within a reinforced concrete shield building. The containment employs the ice condenser pressure-suppression concept. A common auxiliary building adjacent to the containment structure houses the radioactive waste treatment facilities, components of the engineered safety features, and various related auxiliary systems for each unit. The units share a common fuel handling facility that contains a SFP and a new fuel storage facility.

The plant is supplied with electrical power by independent transmission lines from offsite power sources. It has independent and redundant onsite emergency power supplies capable of supplying power to shut down the plant safely or to operate the engineered safety features in the event of an accident. The plant electric power system consists of the main generators, the unit station service transformers, the common station service transformers, the emergency diesel generators (EDGs), the batteries, and the electric distribution system. Under normal operating conditions the main generators supply electrical power through isolated-phase buses to the main step-up transformers and through the unit station service transformers (located adjacent to the turbine building) to the nonsafety auxiliary power system. Offsite electrical power supplies Class 1E circuits through the 161-kilovolt (kV) system via common station service transformers C and D. The primaries of the unit station service transformers are connected to the isolated-phase bus at a point between the generator terminals and the low-voltage connection of the main transformers. During normal operation, station auxiliary power is taken from the main generator through the unit station service transformers and from the 161-kV system through the common station service transformers. The standby onsite power is supplied by four diesel generators.

With the exception of some shared systems, separate and similar safety-related systems and equipment are provided for WBN Units 1 and 2. The major structures at WBN are two reactor buildings, a turbine building, an auxiliary building, a control building, a service and office building, diesel generator buildings, an intake pumping station, and two natural draft cooling towers.

## 1.7    Summary of Outstanding Issues

The staff documented its previous review and conclusions regarding the OL application for WBN Unit 1 in the SER (NUREG-0847, dated June 1982) and its supplements 1 through 20. Based on these reviews, the staff issued an OL for WBN Unit 1 in 1996. In the SER and SSERs 1 through 20, the staff also reviewed and approved certain topics for WBN Unit 2, though no final conclusions were made regarding an OL for WBN Unit 2. To establish the remaining scope and the regulatory framework for the staff's review of an OL for WBN Unit 2, the staff reviewed the SER and SSERs 1 thorough 20. Based on this review, the staff identified "resolved" topics (i.e., out of scope for review) and "open" topics (i.e., in scope for staff review) for WBN Unit 2. Where it was not clear whether the SER topic applied to Unit 2 or not, the staff conservatively identified it as "open" pending further evaluation. It should be noted that these were not technical evaluations of each topic; rather, it was a status review to determine whether the topic was "open" or "resolved." The staff documented this evaluation in SSER 21 as the baseline for resumption of the review of the OL application for Unit 2. Thus, SSER 21 reflects the status of the staff's review of WBN Unit 2 up to 1995. The staff notes that a subsequent, more detailed assessment may find some topics conservatively identified in the initial assessment as "open" that should be redefined as "closed." Conversely, the NRC staff notes that there may be circumstances that could result in the need to reopen some previously closed topic areas that may have been adequately documented and that are considered closed in SSER 21. Such cases will be identified by a footnote in future SSERs to document that previous "open" topics have been recategorized as "closed" without requiring further review, or vice versa.

The SER and SSERs 1 through 20 evaluated the changes to the FSAR until Amendment 91. FSAR Amendment 91 was the initial licensing basis for WBN Unit 1. At this time, the FSAR was applicable to both Units 1 and 2. As part of its updated OL application for WBN Unit 2, TVA split the FSAR Amendment 91 into two separate FSARs for WBN Units 1 and 2. TVA has submitted WBN Unit 2 FSAR Amendments 92 through 102 to address the "open" topics in support of its OL application for WBN Unit 2. These FSAR amendments reflect changes that have occurred since 1995. These FSAR amendments are currently under staff review. The staff's review of these FSAR changes is documented in SSER 22 and subsequent supplements.

Additional general topics (e.g., financial qualifications that were not included in SSER 21, but that should be resolved prior to issuance of an OL) are also identified in SSER 22 and subsequent supplements.

SSER 21 initially provided the table below documenting the status of each SER topic. The relevant document in which the topic was last addressed is shown in parenthesis. This table will be maintained in this and future supplements to reflect the updated status of review for each topic.

## ISSUE STATUS TABLE

| | Issue | Status | | Section | Note |
|---|---|---|---|---|---|
| (1) | Site Envelope | | | 2 | |
| (2) | Geography and Demography | Resolved | (SSER 22) | 2.1 | |
| (3) | Site Location and Description | Resolved | (SER) (SSER 22) | 2.1.1 | 3 |
| (4) | Exclusion Area Authority and Control | Resolved | (SER) (SSER 22) | 2.1.2 | 3 |
| (5) | Population Distribution | Resolved | (SER) (SSER 22) | 2.1.3 | |
| (6) | Conclusions | Resolved | (SER) (SSER 22) | 2.1.4 | |
| (7) | Nearby Industrial, Transportation, and Military Facilities | Resolved | (SSER 22) | 2.2 | |
| (8) | Transportation Routes | Resolved | (SER) (SSER 22) | 2.2.1 | |
| (9) | Nearby Facilities | Resolved | (SER) (SSER 22) | 2.2.2 | |
| (10) | Conclusions | Resolved | (SER) (SSER 22) | 2.2.3 | |
| (11) | Meteorology | | (SER) (SSER 22) | 2.3 | |
| (12) | Regional Climatology | Resolved | (SER) (SSER 22) | 2.3.1 | |
| (13) | Local Meteorology | Resolved | (SER) (SSER 22) | 2.3.2 | |
| (14) | Onsite Meteorological Measurements Program | Resolved | (SER) (SSER 22) (SSER 25) | 2.3.3 | |
| (15) | Short-Term (Accident) Atmospheric Diffusion Estimates | Resolved | (SER) (SSER 14) (SSER 22) | 2.3.4 | |
| (16) | Long-Term (Routine) Diffusion Estimates | Resolved | (SER) (SSER 14) (SSER 22) | 2.3.5 | |
| (17) | Hydrologic Engineering | | | 2.4 | |
| (18) | Introduction | Resolved | (SER) | 2.4.1 | |
| (19) | Hydrologic Description | Resolved | (SER) | 2.4.2 | |
| (20) | Flood Potential | Resolved | (SER) | 2.4.3 | |

| | Issue | Status | | Section | Note |
|---|---|---|---|---|---|
| (21) | Local Intense Precipitation in Plant Area | Resolved | (SER) | 2.4.4 | 1 |
| (22) | Roof Drainage | Resolved | (SER) | 2.4.5 | 1 |
| (23) | Ultimate Heat Sink | Resolved | (SER) | 2.4.6 | |
| (24) | Groundwater | Resolved | (SER) | 2.4.7 | 1 |
| (25) | Design Basis for Subsurface Hydrostatic Loading | Resolved | (SER) (SSER 3) | 2.4.8 | |
| (26) | Transport of Liquid Releases | Resolved | (SER) (SSER 22) | 2.4.9 | 2 |
| (27) | Flooding Protection Requirements | Open (Inspection) | (SER) (SSER 24) | 2.4.10 | |
| (28) | Geological, Seismological, and Geotechnical Engineering | Resolved | (SER) (SSER 24) | 2.5 | |
| (29) | Geology | Resolved | (SER) | 2.5.1 | |
| (30) | Seismology | Resolved | (SER) | 2.5.2 | |
| (31) | Surface Faulting | Resolved | (SER) | 2.5.3 | |
| (32) | Stability of Subsurface Materials and Foundations | Resolved | (SER) (SSER 3) (SSER 9) (SSER 11) | 2.5.4 | |
| (33) | Stability of Slopes | Resolved | (SER) | 2.5.5 | |
| (34) | Embankments and Dams | Resolved | (SER) (SSER 22) | 2.5.6 | |
| (35) | References | | (SER) (SSER 22) | 2.6 | |
| (36) | Design Criteria - Structures, Components, Equipment, and Systems | | | 3 | |
| (37) | Introduction | | | 3.1 | |
| (38) | Conformance With General Design Criteria | Resolved | (SER) | 3.1.1 | |
| (39) | Conformance With Industry Codes and Standards | Resolved | (SER) | 3.1.2 | |
| (40) | Classification of Structures, Systems and Components | Resolved | (SSER 14) (SSER 22) | 3.2 | |
| (41) | Seismic Classifications | Resolved | (SER) (SSER 3) (SSER 5) (SSER 6) (SSER 8) | 3.2.1 | |
| (42) | System Quality Group Classification | Open (NRR) | (SER) (SSER 3) (SSER 6) (SSER 7) (SSER 9) (SSER 22) | 3.2.2 | |
| (43) | Wind and Tornado Loadings | | | 3.3 | |
| (44) | Wind Loading | Resolved | (SER) | 3.3.1 | |

|  | Issue | Status | | Section | Note |
|---|---|---|---|---|---|
| (45) | Tornado Loading | Resolved | (SER) | 3.3.2 | |
| (46) | Flood Level (Flood) Design | | | 3.4 | |
| (47) | Flood Protection | Resolved | (SER) | 3.4.1 | |
| (48) | Missile Protection | | | 3.5 | |
| (49) | Missile Selection and Description | Resolved | (SER) (SSER 9) (SSER 14) (SSER 22) | 3.5.1 | |
| (50) | Structures, Systems, and Components to be Protected from Externally Generated Missiles | Resolved | (SER) (SSER 2) (SSER 22) | 3.5.2 | |
| (51) | Barrier Design Procedures | Resolved | (SER) | 3.5.3 | |
| (52) | Protection Against the Dynamic Effects Associated with the Postulated Rupture of Piping | Open (NRR) | (SER) (SSER 6) (SSER 11) | 3.6 | |
| (53) | Plant Design for Protection Against Postulated Piping Failures in Fluid System Outside Containment | Resolved | (SER) (SSER 14) (SSER 22) | 3.6.1 | |
| (54) | Determination of Break Locations and Dynamic Effects Associated with the Postulated Rupture of Piping | Resolved | (SER) (SSER 14) (SSER 22) | 3.6.2 | 3 |
| (55) | Leak-Before-Break Evaluation Procedures | Resolved | (SSER 5) (SSER 12) (SSER 22) (SSER 24) | 3.6.3 | |
| (56) | Seismic Design | Resolved | (SER) (SSER 6) | 3.7 | 2 |
| (57) | Seismic Input | Resolved | (SER) (SSER 6) (SSER 9) (SSER 16) | 3.7.1 | 2 |
| (58) | Seismic Analysis | Resolved | (SER) (SSER 6) (SSER 8) (SSER 11) (SSER 16) | 3.7.2 | 2 |
| (59) | Seismic Subsystem Analysis | Resolved | (SER) (SSER 6) (SSER 7) (SSER 8) (SSER 9) (SSER 12) (SSER 22) | 3.7.3 | |
| (60) | Seismic Instrumentation | Resolved | (SER) | 3.7.4 | 1 |
| (61) | Design of Seismic Category I Structures | Resolved | (SER) (SSER 9) | 3.8 | 2 |
| (62) | Steel Containment | Resolved | (SER) (SSER 3) | 3.8.1 | |

| | Issue | Status | | Section | Note |
|---|---|---|---|---|---|
| (63) | Concrete and Structural Steel Internal Structures | Resolved | (SER) (SSER 7) | 3.8.2 | |
| (64) | Other Seismic Category I Structures | Open (NRR) | (SER) (SSER 14) (SSER 16) | 3.8.3 | |
| (65) | Foundations | Resolved | (SER) | 3.8.4 | |
| (66) | Mechanical Systems and Components | Resolved | (SER) | 3.9 | |
| (67) | Special Topics for Mechanical Components | Resolved | (SER) (SSER 6) (SSER 13) (SSER 22) | 3.9.1 | |
| (68) | Dynamic Testing and Analysis of Systems, Components, and Equipment | Resolved | (SER) (SSER 14) (SSER 22) | 3.9.2 | |
| (69) | ASME Code Class 1, 2, and 3 Components, Component Structures, and Core Support Structures | Resolved | (SER) (SSER 3) (SSER 4) (SSER 6) (SSER 7) (SSER 8) (SSER 15) (SSER 22) | 3.9.3 | |
| (70) | Control Rod Drive Systems | Resolved | (SER) | 3.9.4 | |
| (71) | Reactor Pressure Vessel Internals | Open | (SER) (SSER 23) | 3.9.5 | |
| (72) | Inservice Testing of Pumps and Valves | Open (NRR) | (SER) (SSER 5) (SSER 12) (SSER 14) (SSER 18) (SSER 20) (SSER 22) | 3.9.6 | |
| (73) | Seismic and Dynamic Qualification of Seismic Category I Mechanical and Electrical Equipment | Resolved | (SER) (SSER 1) (SSER 3) (SSER 4) (SSER 5) (SSER 6) (SSER 8) (SSER 9) (SSER 23) | 3.10 | |
| (74) | Environmental Qualification of Mechanical and Electrical Equipment | Open (NRR) | (SSER 15) (SSER 22) | 3.11 | |
| (75) | Threaded Fasteners — ASME Code Class 1, 2, and 3 | Resolved | (SSER 22) | 3.13 | |
| (76) | Reactor | | | 4 | |

| | Issue | Status | Section | Note |
|---|---|---|---|---|
| (77) | Introduction | | (SER) | 4.1 |
| | | | (SSER 23) | |
| (78) | Fuel System Design | | (SSER 23) | 4.2 |
| (79) | Description | Resolved | (SER) | 4.2.1 |
| | | | (SSER 13) | |
| | | | (SSER 23) | |
| (80) | Thermal Performance | Open (NRR) | (SER) | 4.2.2 |
| | | | (SSER 2) | |
| | | | (SSER 23) | |
| (81) | Mechanical Performance | Resolved | (SER) | 4.2.3 |
| | | | (SSER 2) | |
| | | | (SSER 10) | |
| | | | (SSER 13) | |
| | | | (SSER 23) | |
| (82) | Surveillance | | (SER) | 4.2.4 |
| (83) | Fuel Design Considerations | Resolved | (SER) | 4.2.5 |
| | | | (SSER 23) | |
| (84) | Nuclear Design | | (SSER 23) | 4.3 |
| (85) | Design Basis | Resolved | (SER) | 4.3.1 |
| | | | (SSER 13) | |
| | | | (SSER 23) | |
| (86) | Design Description | Resolved | (SER) | 4.3.2 |
| | | | (SSER 13) | |
| | | | (SSER 15) | |
| | | | (SSER 23) | |
| (87) | Analytical Methods | Resolved | (SER) | 4.3.3 |
| | | | (SSER 23) | |
| (88) | Summary of Evaluation Findings | Resolved | (SER) | 4.3.4 |
| | | | (SSER 23) | |
| (89) | Thermal-Hydraulic Design | | (SSER 23) | 4.4 |
| (90) | Performance in Safety Criteria | Resolved | (SER) | 4.4.1 |
| | | | (SSER 23) | |
| (91) | Design Bases | Resolved | (SER) | 4.4.2 |
| | | | (SSER 12) | |
| | | | (SSER 23) | |
| (92) | Thermal-Hydraulic Design Methodology | Resolved | (SER) | 4.4.3 |
| | | | (SSER 6) | |
| | | | (SSER 8) | |
| | | | (SSER 12) | |
| | | | (SSER 13) | |
| | | | (SSER 16) | |
| | | | SE dated 6/13/89 | |
| | | | (SSER 23) | |
| (93) | Operating Abnormalities | Resolved | (SER) | 4.4.4 |
| | | | (SSER 13) | |
| | | | (SSER 23) | |

| | Issue | Status | | Section | Note |
|---|---|---|---|---|---|
| (94) | Loose Parts Monitoring System | Resolved | (SER) (SSER 3) (SSER 5) (SSER 16) (SSER 23) | 4.4.5 | |
| (95) | Thermal-Hydraulic Comparison | Resolved | (SER) (SSER 23) | 4.4.6 | |
| (96) | N-1 Loop Operation | Resolved | (SER) (SSER 23) | 4.4.7 | |
| (97) | Instrumentation for Inadequate Core Cooling Detection (TMI Action Item II.F.2) | Open (NRR) | (SER) (SSER 10) (SSER 23) | 4.4.8 | |
| (98) | Summary and Conclusion | Open (NRR) | (SER) (SSER 23) | 4.4.9 | |
| (99) | Reactor Materials | | | 4.5 | |
| (100) | Control Rod Drive Structural Materials | Resolved | (SER) | 4.5.1 | 1 |
| (101) | Reactor Internals and Core Support Materials | Resolved | (SER) | 4.5.2 | |
| (102) | Functional Design of Reactivity Control Systems | Resolved | (SER) (SSER 23) | 4.6 | |
| (103) | Reactor Coolant System and Connected Systems | | | 5 | |
| (104) | Summary Description | Resolved | (SER) (SSER 5) (SSER 6) | 5.1 | 2 |
| (105) | Integrity of Reactor Coolant Pressure Boundary | | | 5.2 | |
| (106) | Compliance with Codes and Code Cases | Resolved | (SER) (SSER 22) | 5.2.1 | |
| (107) | Overpressurization Protection | Resolved | (SER) (SSER 2) (SSER 15) (SSER 24) | 5.2.2 | |
| (108) | Reactor Coolant Pressure Boundary Materials | Resolved | (SER) (SSER 22) | 5.2.3 | |
| (109) | Reactor Coolant System Pressure Boundary Inservice Inspection and Testing | Open (NRR) | (SER) (SSER 10) (SSER 12) (SSER 15) (SSER 16) (SSER 23) | 5.2.4 | |
| (110) | Reactor Coolant Pressure Boundary Leakage Detection | Resolved | (SER) (SSER 9) (SSER 11) (SSER 12) (SSER 22) | 5.2.5 | |
| (111) | Reactor Vessel and Internals Modeling | | | 5.2.6 | |

| Issue | | Status | | Section | Note |
|-------|---|--------|---|---------|------|
| (112) | Reactor Vessel | | | 5.3 | |
| (113) | Reactor Vessel Materials | Resolved | (SER) | 5.3.1 | |
| | | | (SSER 11) | | |
| | | | (SSER 14) | | |
| | | | (SSER 22) | | |
| | | | (SSER 25) | | |
| (114) | Pressure-Temperature Limits | Resolved | (SER) | 5.3.2 | |
| | | | (SSER 16) | | |
| | | | (SSER 22) | | |
| | | | (SSER 25) | | |
| (115) | Reactor Vessel Integrity | Open (NRR) | (SER) | 5.3.3 | |
| | | | (SSER 22) | | |
| (116) | Component and Subsystem Design | | | 5.4 | |
| (117) | Reactor Coolant Pumps | Resolved | (SER) | 5.4.1 | 2 |
| | | | (SSER 22) | | |
| (118) | Steam Generators | Resolved | (SER) | 5.4.2 | |
| | | | (SSER 1) | | |
| | | | (SSER 4) | | |
| | | | (SSER 22) | | |
| (119) | Residual Heat Removal System | Resolved | (SER) | 5.4.3 | |
| | | | (SSER 2) | | |
| | | | (SSER 5) | | |
| | | | (SSER 10) | | |
| | | | (SSER 11) | | |
| | | | (SSER 23) | | |
| (120) | Pressurizer Relief Tank | Resolved | (SER) | 5.4.4 | |
| | | | (SSER 22) | | |
| (121) | Reactor Coolant System Vents (TMI Action Item II.B.1) | Open (Inspection) | (SER) | 5.4.5 | |
| | | | (SSER 2) | | |
| | | | (SSER 5) | | |
| | | | (SSER 12) | | |
| | | | (SSER 23) | | |
| (122) | Engineered Safety Features | | | 6 | |
| (123) | Engineered Safety Feature Materials | | | 6.1 | |
| (124) | Metallic Materials | Open | (SER) | 6.1.1 | |
| | | | (SSER 23) | | |
| (125) | Organic Materials | Resolved | (SER) | 6.1.2 | |
| | | | (SSER 22) | | |
| (126) | Postaccident Emergency Cooling Water Chemistry | Resolved | (SER) | 6.1.3 | |
| | | | (SSER 22) | | |
| (127) | Containment Systems | | | 6.2 | |

| | Issue | Status | | Section | Note |
|---|---|---|---|---|---|
| (128) | Containment Functional Design | Resolved | (SER) (SSER 3) (SSER 5) (SSER 7) (SSER 12) (SSER 14) (SSER 15) (SSER 22) | 6.2.1 | |
| (129) | Containment Heat Removal Systems | Resolved | (SER) (SSER 7) (SSER 22) | 6.2.2 | |
| (130) | Secondary Containment Functional Design | Resolved | (SER) (SSER 18) (SSER 22) | 6.2.3 | |
| (131) | Containment Isolation Systems | Resolved | (SER) (SSER 3) (SSER 5) (SSER 7) (SSER 12) (SSER 22) | 6.2.4 | |
| (132) | Combustible Gas Control Systems | Resolved | (SER) (SSER 4) (SSER 5) (SSER 8) (SSER 22) | 6.2.5 | |
| (133) | Containment Leakage Testing | Open (NRR) | (SER) (SSER 4) (SSER 5) (SSER 19) (SSER 22) | 6.2.6 | |
| (134) | Fracture Prevention of Containment Pressure Boundary | Resolved | (SER) (SSER 4) (SSER 23) | 6.2.7 | 1 |
| (135) | Emergency Core Cooling System | Resolved | (SER) | 6.3 | 1 |
| (136) | System Design | Open (NRR) | (SER) (SSER 6) (SSER 7) (SSER 11) | 6.3.1 | |
| (137) | Evaluation | Resolved | (SER) (SSER 5) | 6.3.2 | 1 |
| (138) | Testing | Open (NRR) | (SER) (SSER 2) (SSER 9) | 6.3.3 | |
| (139) | Performance Evaluation | Resolved | (SER) | 6.3.4 | |
| (140) | Conclusions | Open (NRR) | (SER) | 6.3.5 | |

| | Issue | Status | | Section | Note |
|---|---|---|---|---|---|
| (141) | Control Room Habitability | Resolved | (SER) (SSER 5) (SSER 11) (SSER 16) (SSER 18 (SSER 22) | 6.4 | |
| (142) | Engineered Safety Feature (ESF) Filter Systems | | | 6.5 | |
| (143) | ESF Atmosphere Cleanup System | Resolved | (SER) (SSER 5) (SSER 22) | 6.5.1 | |
| (144) | Fission Product Cleanup System | Resolved | (SER) | 6.5.2 | 1 |
| (145) | Fission Product Control System | Open (NRR) | (SER) (SSER 22) | 6.5.3 | |
| (146) | Ice Condenser as a Fission Product Cleanup System | Resolved | (SER) | 6.5.4 | 1 |
| (147) | Inservice Inspection of Class 2 and 3 Components | Open (NRR) | (SER) (SSER 10) (SSER 12) (SSER 15) (SSER 23) | 6.6 | |
| (148) | Instrumentation and Controls | | | 7 | |
| (149) | Introduction | | | 7.1 | |
| (150) | General | Resolved | (SER) (SSER 13) (SSER 16) (SSER 23) | 7.1.1 | |
| (151) | Comparison with Other Plants | Resolved | (SER) (SSER 23) | 7.1.2 | 1 |
| (152) | Design Criteria | Resolved | (SER) (SSER 4) (SSER 15) (SSER 23) | 7.1.3 | |
| (153) | Reactor Trip System | Resolved | (SER) | 7.2 | |
| (154) | System Description | Open (NRR) | (SER) (SSER 13) (SSER 15) (SSER 23) | 7.2.1 | |
| (155) | Manual Trip Switches | Resolved | (SER) (SSER 23) | 7.2.2 | 1 |
| (156) | Testing of Reactor Trip Breaker Shunt Coils | Resolved | (SER) (SSER 23) | 7.2.3 | 1 |
| (157) | Anticipatory Trips | Resolved | (SER) (SSER 23) | 7.2.4 | |
| (158) | Steam Generator Water Level Trip | Resolved | (SER) (SSER 2) (SSER 14) (SSER 23) | 7.2.5 | |

| | Issue | Status | | Section | Note |
|---|---|---|---|---|---|
| (159) | Conclusions | Resolved | (SER) (SSER 13) (SSER 23) | 7.2.6 | |
| (160) | Engineered Safety Features System | Open (NRR) | (SER) (SSER 13) | 7.3 | |
| (161) | System Description | Resolved | (SER) (SSER 13) (SSER 14) (SSER 23) | 7.3.1 | |
| (162) | Containment Sump Level Measurement | Resolved | (SER) (SSER 2) (SSER 23) | 7.3.2 | |
| (163) | Auxiliary Feedwater Initiation and Control | Resolved | (SER) (SSER 23) | 7.3.3 | 1 |
| (164) | Failure Modes and Effects Analysis | Resolved | (SER) (SSER 23) | 7.3.4 | |
| (165) | IE Bulletin 80-06 | Resolved | (SER) (SSER 3) (SSER 23) | 7.3.5 | |
| (166) | Conclusions | Resolved | (SER) (SSER 13) (SSER 23) | 7.3.6 | |
| (167) | Systems Required for Safe Shutdown | | | 7.4 | |
| (168) | System Description | Resolved | (SER) (SSER 23) | 7.4.1 | |
| (169) | Safe Shutdown from Auxiliary Control Room | Resolved | (SER) (SSER 7) (SSER 23) | 7.4.2 | |
| (170) | Conclusions | Resolved | (SER) (SSER 23) | 7.4.3 | |
| (171) | Safety-Related Display Instrumentation | | | 7.5 | |
| (172) | Display Systems | Resolved | (SER) (SSER 23) | 7.5.1 | |
| (173) | Postaccident Monitoring System | Open (Inspection) | (SER) (SSER 7) (SSER 9) (SSER 14) (SSER 15) (SSER 23) (SSER 25) | 7.5.2 | |
| (174) | IE Bulletin 79-27 | Open (Inspection) | (SER) (SSER 23) | 7.5.3 | |
| (175) | Conclusions | Open (Inspection) | (SER) | 7.5.4 | |
| (176) | All Other Systems Required for Safety | | | 7.6 | |

| | Issue | Status | | Section | Note |
|---|---|---|---|---|---|
| (177) | Loose Part Monitoring System | Resolved | (SER) (SSER 23) (SSER 24) | 7.6.1 | |
| (178) | Residual Heat Removal System Bypass Valves | Resolved | (SER) (SSER 23) | 7.6.2 | |
| (179) | Upper Head Injection Manual Control | Resolved | (SER) (SSER 23) | 7.6.3 | |
| (180) | Protection Against Spurious Actuation of Motor-Operated Valves | Resolved | (SER) (SSER 23) | 7.6.4 | |
| (181) | Overpressure Protection during Low Temperature Operation | Resolved | (SER) (SSER 4) (SSER 23) | 7.6.5 | |
| (182) | Valve Power Lockout | Resolved | (SER) (SSER 23) | 7.6.6 | |
| (183) | Cold Leg Accumulator Valve Interlocks and Position Indication | Resolved | (SER) (SSER 23) | 7.6.7 | |
| (184) | Automatic Switchover From Injection to Recirculation Mode | Resolved | (SER) (SSER 23) | 7.6.8 | |
| (185) | Conclusions | Resolved | (SER) (SSER 4) | 7.6.9 | |
| (186) | Control Systems Not Required for Safety | | | 7.7 | |
| (187) | System Description | Open (NRR) | (SER) (SSER 23) (SSER 24) (SSER 25) | 7.7.1 | |
| (188) | Safety System Status Monitoring System | Resolved | (SER) (SSER 7) (SSER 13) (SSER 23) | 7.7.2 | |
| (189) | Volume Control Tank Level Control System | Resolved | (SER) (SSER 23) | 7.7.3 | |
| (190) | Pressurizer and Steam Generator Overfill | Resolved | (SER) (SSER 23) | 7.7.4 | |
| (191) | IE Information Notice 79-22 | Resolved | (SER) (SSER 23) | 7.7.5 | |
| (192) | Multiple Control System Failures | Resolved | (SER) (SSER 23) | 7.7.6 | |
| (193) | Conclusions | Resolved | (SER) | 7.7.7 | |
| (194) | Anticipated Transient Without Scram Mitigation System Actuation Circuitry (AMSAC) | Resolved | (SSER 9) (SSER 14) (SSER 23) | 7.7.8 | |
| (195) | NUREG-0737 Items | Resolved | (SER) (SSER 23) | 7.8 | |
| (196) | Relief and Safety Valve Position Indication (TMI Action Item II.D.3) | Open (Inspection) | (SER) (SSER 5) (SSER 14) (SSER 23) | 7.8.1 | |

| | Issue | Status | | Section | Note |
|---|---|---|---|---|---|
| (197) | Auxiliary Feedwater System Initiation and Flow Indication (TMI Action Item II.E.1.2) | Open (Inspection) | (SER) (SSER 23) | 7.8.2 | |
| (198) | Proportional Integral Derivative Control Modification (TMI Action Item II.K.3.9) | Open (Inspection) | (SER) (SSER 23) | 7.8.3 | |
| (199) | Proposed Anticipatory Trip Modification (TMI Action Item II.K.3.10) | Resolved | (SER) (SSER 4) (SSER 23) | 7.8.4 | |
| (200) | Confirm Existence of Anticipatory Reactor Trip Upon Turbine Trip (TMI Action Item II.K.3.12) | Resolved | (SER) (SSER 23) | 7.8.5 | |
| (201) | Data Communication Systems | | (SSER 23) | 7.9 | |
| (202) | Electric Power Systems | | | 8 | |
| (203) | General | Open (NRR) | (SER) (SSER 22) (SSER 24) | 8.1 | |
| (204) | Offsite Power System | | (SER) (SSER 22) | 8.2 | |
| (205) | Compliance with GDC 5 | Open (NRR) | (SER) (SSER 13) (SSER 22) | 8.2.1 | |
| (206) | Compliance with GDC 17 | Open (NRR) | (SER) (SSER 2) (SSER 3) (SSER 13) (SSER 14) (SSER 15 (SSER 22) | 8.2.2 | |
| (207) | Compliance with GDC 18 | Resolved | (SER) (SSER 22) | 8.2.3 | |
| (208) | Evaluation Findings | Open (NRR) | (SER) (SSER 22) | 8.2.4 | |
| (209) | Onsite Power Systems | Resolved | (SER) (SSER 10) (SSER 19) (SSER 22) | 8.3 | |
| (210) | Onsite AC Power System Compliance with GDC 17 | Open (NRR) | (SER) (SSER 2) (SSER 7) (SSER 9) (SSER 10) (SSER 13) (SSER 14) (SSER 18) (SSER 20) (SSER 22) | 8.3.1 | |

| | Issue | Status | | Section | Note |
|---|---|---|---|---|---|
| (211) | Onsite DC System Compliance with GDC 17 | Open (NRR) | (SER) (SSER 2) (SSER 3) (SSER 13) (SSER 14) (SSER 22) | 8.3.2 | |
| (212) | Common Electrical Features and Requirements | Resolved | (SER) (SSER 2) (SSER 3) (SSER 7) (SSER 13) (SSER 14) (SSER 15) (SSER 16) (SSER 22) | 8.3.3 | |
| (213) | Evaluation Findings | Open (NRR) | (SER) (SSER 2) (SSER 3) (SSER 7) (SSER 13) (SSER 14) (SSER 15) (SSER 16) (SSER 22) | 8.3.4 | |
| (214) | Station Blackout | Open (NRR) | (SSER 22) | 8.4 | |
| (215) | Auxiliary Systems | Resolved | (SER) (SSER 10) | 9 | |
| (216) | Fuel Storage Facility | | | 9.1 | |
| (217) | New-Fuel Storage | Resolved | (SER) | 9.1.1 | 1 |
| (218) | Spent-Fuel Storage | Resolved | (SER) (SSER 5) (SSER 15) (SSER 16) (SSER 22) | 9.1.2 | |
| (219) | Spent Fuel Pool Cooling and Cleanup System | Open (NRR) | (SER) (SSER 11) (SSER 15) (SSER 23) | 9.1.3 | |
| (220) | Fuel-Handling System | Resolved | (SER) (SSER 3) (SSER 13) (SSER 22) (SSER 24) | 9.1.4 | |
| (221) | Water Systems | | | 9.2 | |
| (222) | Essential Raw Cooling Water and Raw Cooling Water System | Open (NRR) | (SER) (SSER 9) (SSER 10) (SSER 18) (SSER 23) | 9.2.1 | |

| | Issue | Status | | Section | Note |
|---|---|---|---|---|---|
| (223) | Component Cooling System (Reactor Auxiliaries Cooling Water System) | Open (NRR) | (SER) (SSER 5) (SSER 23) | 9.2.2 | |
| (224) | Demineralized Water Makeup System | Resolved | (SER) (SSER 22) | 9.2.3 | |
| (225) | Potable and Sanitary Water Systems | Resolved | (SER) (SSER 9) (SSER 22) | 9.2.4 | |
| (226) | Ultimate Heat Sink | Open (NRR) | (SER) (SSER 23) | 9.2.5 | |
| (227) | Condensate Storage Facilities | Resolved | (SER) (SSER 12) (SSER 22) | 9.2.6 | |
| (228) | Process Auxiliaries | | | 9.3 | |
| (229) | Compressed Air System | Resolved | (SER) (SSER 22) | 9.3.1 | 1 |
| (230) | Process Sampling System | Resolved | (SER) (SSER 3) (SSER 5) (SSER 14) (SSER 16) (SSER 24) | 9.3.2 | |
| (231) | Equipment and Floor Drainage System | Resolved | (SER) (SSER 22) | 9.3.3 | 3 |
| (232) | Chemical and Volume Control System | Resolved | (SER) (SSER 22) | 9.3.4 | 3 |
| (233) | Heat Tracing | | (SSER 22) | 9.3.8 | |
| (234) | Heating, Ventilation, and Air Conditioning Systems | | | 9.4 | |
| (235) | Control Room Area Ventilation System | Resolved | (SER) (SSER 9) (SSER 22) | 9.4.1 | |
| (236) | Fuel-Handling Area Ventilation System | Resolved | (SER) (SSER 22) | 9.4.2 | |
| (237) | Auxiliary Building and Radwaste Area Ventilation System | Resolved | (SER) (SSER 22) | 9.4.3 | |
| (238) | Turbine Building Area Ventilation System | Resolved | (SER) (SSER 22) | 9.4.4 | |
| (239) | Engineered Safety Features Ventilation System | Resolved | (SER) (SSER 9) (SSER 10) (SSER 11) (SSER 14) (SSER 16) (SSER 19) (SSER 22) | 9.4.5 | |
| (240) | Reactor Building Purge Ventilation System | | (SSER 22) | 9.4.6 | |
| (241) | Containment Air Cooling System | | (SSER 22) | 9.4.7 | |

| | Issue | Status | | Section | Note |
|---|---|---|---|---|---|
| (242) | Condensate Demineralizer Waste Evaporator Building Environmental Control System | | (SSER 22) | 9.4.8 | |
| (243) | Other Auxiliary Systems | | | 9.5 | |
| (244) | Fire Protection | Resolved | (SER) (SSER 10) (SSER 18) (SSER 19) | 9.5.1 | |
| (245) | Communications System | Resolved | (SER) (SSER 5) | 9.5.2 | 1 |
| (246) | Lighting System | Resolved | (SER) (SSER 22) | 9.5.3 | |
| (247) | Emergency Diesel Engine Fuel Oil Storage and Transfer System | Resolved | (SER) (SSER 5) (SSER 9) (SSER 10) (SSER 11) (SSER 12) (SSER 22) | 9.5.4 | 2 |
| (248) | Emergency Diesel Engine Cooling Water System | Resolved | (SER) (SSER 5) (SSER 11) | 9.5.5 | 1 |
| (249) | Emergency Diesel Engine Starting Systems | Resolved | (SER) (SSER 5) (SSER 10) (SSER 22) | 9.5.6 | 2 |
| (250) | Emergency Diesel Engine Lubricating Oil System | Resolved | (SER) (SSER 3) (SSER 5) (SSER 10) (SSER 22) | 9.5.7 | 2 |
| (251) | Emergency Diesel Engine Combustion Air Intake and Exhaust System | Resolved | (SER) (SSER 5) (SSER 10) (SSER 22) | 9.5.8 | 2 |
| (252) | Steam and Power Conversion System | | | 10 | |
| (253) | Summary Description | Resolved | (SER) | 10.1 | |
| (254) | Turbine Generator | Open (NRR) | (SER) (SSER 5) | 10.2 | |
| (255) | Turbine Generator Design | Resolved | (SER) (SSER 12) (SSER 22) | 10.2.1 | |
| (256) | Turbine Disc Integrity | Resolved | (SER) (SSER 23) | 10.2.2 | |
| (257) | Main Steam Supply System | Resolved | (SER) | 10.3 | |
| (258) | Main Steam Supply System (Up to and Including the Main Steam Isolation Valves) | Resolved | (SER) (SSER 19) (SSER 22) | 10.3.1 | |

| | Issue | Status | | Section | Note |
|---|---|---|---|---|---|
| (259) | Main Steam Supply System | Resolved | (SER) (SSER 22) | 10.3.2 | 2 |
| (260) | Steam and Feedwater System Materials | Resolved | (SER) (SSER 22) | 10.3.3 | |
| (261) | Secondary Water Chemistry | Resolved | (SER) (SSER 5) (SSER 22) | 10.3.4 | |
| (262) | Other Features | | | 10.4 | |
| (263) | Main Condenser | Resolved | (SER) (SSER 9) (SSER 22) | 10.4.1 | |
| (264) | Main Condenser Evacuation System | Resolved | (SER) (SSER 22) | 10.4.2 | |
| (265) | Turbine Gland Sealing System | Resolved | (SER) (SSER 22) | 10.4.3 | |
| (266) | Turbine Bypass System | Resolved | (SER) (SSER 5) (SSER 22) | 10.4.4 | |
| (267) | Condenser Circulating Water System | Resolved | (SER) (SSER 22) | 10.4.5 | |
| (268) | Condensate Cleanup System | Open (NRR) | (SER) (SSER 22) | 10.4.6 | |
| (269) | Condensate and Feedwater Systems | Resolved | (SER) (SSER 14) (SSER 22) | 10.4.7 | |
| (270) | Steam Generator Blowdown System | Resolved | (SER) (SSER 22) (SSER 24) | 10.4.8 | |
| (271) | Auxiliary Feedwater System | Resolved | (SER) (SSER 14) (SSER 23) (SSER 24) | 10.4.9 | |
| (272) | Heater Drains and Vents | | (SSER 22) | 10.4.10 | |
| (273) | Steam Generator Wet Layup System | | (SSER 22) | 10.4.11 | |
| (274) | Radioactive Waste Management | | | 11 | |
| (275) | Summary Description | Resolved | (SER) (SSER 16) (SSER 24) | 11.1 | 2 |
| (276) | Liquid Waste Management | Resolved | (SER) (SSER 4) (SSER 16) (SSER 24) | 11.2 | |
| (277) | Gaseous Waste Management | Resolved | (SER) (SSER 8) (SSER 16) (SSER 24) (SSER 25) | 11.3 | |

| | Issue | Status | | Section | Note |
|---|---|---|---|---|---|
| (278) | Solid Waste Management System | Resolved | (SER) (SSER 16) (SSER 24) | 11.4 | |
| (279) | Process and Effluent Radiological Monitoring and Sampling Systems | Resolved | (SER) (SSER 16) (SSER 20) (SSER 24) | 11.5 | |
| (280) | Evaluation Findings | Resolved | (SER) (SSER 8) (SSER 16) | 11.6 | |
| (281) | NUREG-0737 Items | Open (NRR) | (SER) | 11.7 | |
| (282) | Wide-Range Noble Gas, Iodine, and Particulate Effluent Monitors (TMI Action Items II.F.1(1) and II.F.1(2)) | Open (Inspection) | (SER) (SSER 5) (SSER 6) | 11.7.1 | |
| (283) | Primary Coolant Outside Containment (TMI Action item III.D.1.1) | Open (NRR) | (SER) (SSER 5) (SSER 6) (SSER 10) (SSER 16) | 11.7.2 | |
| (284) | Radiation Protection | | | 12 | |
| (285) | General | Resolved | (SER) (SSER 10) (SSER 14) (SSER 24) | 12.1 | |
| (286) | Ensuring that Occupational Radiation Doses Are As Low As Reasonably Achievable (ALARA) | Resolved | (SER) (SSER 14) (SSER 24) | 12.2 | 2 |
| (287) | Radiation Sources | Resolved | (SER) (SSER 14) (SSER 24) | 12.3 | |
| (288) | Radiation Protection Design Features | Open (NRR) | (SER) (SSER 10) (SSER 14) (SSER 18) (SSER 24) | 12.4 | |
| (289) | Dose Assessment | Open (NRR) | (SER) (SSER 14) (SSER 24) | 12.5 | |
| (290) | Health Physics Program | Open (NRR) | (SER) (SSER 10) (SSER 14) (SSER 24) | 12.6 | |
| (291) | NUREG-0737 Items | | | 12.7 | |
| (292) | Plant Shielding (TMI Action Item II.B.2) | Open (NRR) | (SER) (SSER 14) (SSER 16) (SSER 24) | 12.7.1 | |
| (293) | High Range In-Containment Monitor (TMI Action Item II.F.1.(3)) | Open (NRR) | (SER) (SSER 5) | 12.7.2 | |

| | Issue | Status | | Section | Note |
|---|---|---|---|---|---|
| (294) | In-Plant Radioiodine Monitor (TMI Action Item II.D.3.3) | Open (NRR) | (SER) (SSER 16) | 12.7.3 | |
| (295) | Conduct of Operations | | | 13 | |
| (296) | Organization Structure of the Applicant | Resolved | (SER) (SSER 16) (SSER 22) | 13.1 | |
| (297) | Management and Technical Organization | Resolved | (SER) | 13.1.1 | |
| (298) | Corporate Organization and Technical Support | Resolved | (SER) | 13.1.2 | |
| (299) | Plant Staff Organization | Resolved | (SER) (SSER 8) (SSER 22) (SSER 25) | 13.1.3 | |
| (300) | Training | | | 13.2 | |
| (301) | Licensed Operator Training Program | Resolved | (SER) (SSER 9) (SSER 10) (SSER 22) | 13.2.1 | |
| (302) | Training for Non-licensed Personnel | Resolved | (SER) | 13.2.2 | |
| (303) | Emergency Preparedness Evaluation | | | 13.3 | |
| (304) | Introduction | Open (NRR) | (SER) (SSER 13) (SSER 20) | 13.3.1 | |
| (305) | Evaluation of the Emergency Plan | Open (NRR) | (SER) (SSER 13) (SSER 20) (SSER 22) | 13.3.2 | |
| (306) | Conclusions | Open (NRR) | (SER) (SSER 13) (SSER 20) (SSER 22) | 13.3.3 | |
| (307) | Review and Audit | Resolved | (SER) (SSER 8) (SSER 22) | 13.4 | |
| (308) | Plant Procedures | Resolved | (SER) (SSER 22) | 13.5 | |
| (309) | Administrative Procedures | Resolved | (SER) (SSER 22) | 13.5.1 | |
| (310) | Operating and Maintenance Procedures | Resolved | (SER) (SSER 9) (SSER 10) (SSER 22) | 13.5.2 | |
| (311) | NUREG-0737 Items | Resolved | (SER) (SSER 3) (SSER 16) (SSER 22) | 13.5.3 | |

| | Issue | Status | | Section | Note |
|---|---|---|---|---|---|
| (312) | Physical Security Plan | Resolved | (SER) | 13.6 | |
| | | | (SSER 1) | | |
| | | | (SSER 10) | | |
| | | | (SSER 15) | | |
| | | | (SSER 20) | | |
| | | | (SSER 22) | | |
| (313) | Introduction | | (SSER 22) | 13.6.1 | |
| (314) | Summary of Application | | (SSER 22) | 13.6.2 | |
| (315) | Regulatory Basis | | (SSER 22) | 13.6.3 | |
| (316) | Technical Evaluation | | (SSER 22) | 13.6.4 | |
| (317) | Conclusions | | (SSER 22) | 13.6.5 | |
| (317a) | Cyber Security Plan | Resolved | (SSER 24) | 13.6.6 | |
| (318) | Initial Test Program | Resolved | (SER) | 14 | |
| | | | (SSER 3) | | |
| | | | (SSER 5) | | |
| | | | (SSER 7) | | |
| | | | (SSER 9) | | |
| | | | (SSER 10) | | |
| | | | (SSER 12) | | |
| | | | (SSER 14) | | |
| | | | (SSER 16) | | |
| | | | (SSER 18) | | |
| | | | (SSER 19) | | |
| | | | (SSER 23) | | |
| (319) | Accident Analyses | | | 15 | |
| (320) | General Discussion | Resolved | (SER) | 15.1 | |
| (321) | Normal Operation and Anticipated Transients | Open (NRR) | (SER) | 15.2 | |
| (322) | Loss-of-Cooling Transients | Resolved | (SER) | 15.2.1 | |
| | | | (SSER 13) | | |
| | | | (SSER 14) | | |
| | | | (SSER 24) | | |
| (323) | Increased Cooling Inventory Transients | Resolved | (SER) | 15.2.2 | |
| | | | (SSER 24) | | |
| (324) | Change in Inventory Transients | Resolved | (SER) | 15.2.3 | |
| | | | (SSER 18) | | |
| | | | (SSER 24) | | |
| (325) | Reactivity and Power Distribution Anomalies | Open (NRR) | (SER) | 15.2.4 | |
| | | | (SSER 4) | | |
| | | | (SSER 7) | | |
| | | | (SSER 13) | | |
| | | | (SSER 14) | | |
| | | | (SSER 24) | | |
| (326) | Conclusions | Resolved | (SER) | 15.2.5 | |
| | | | (SSER 4) | | |
| (327) | Limiting Accidents | Resolved | (SER) | 15.3 | |

| | Issue | Status | | Section | Note |
|---|---|---|---|---|---|
| (328) | Loss-of-Coolant Accident (LOCA) | Resolved | (SER)<br>(SSER 12)<br>(SSER 15)<br>(SSER 24) | 15.3.1 | |
| (329) | Steamline Break | Resolved | (SER)<br>(SSER 3)<br>(SSER 14)<br>(SSER 24) | 15.3.2 | |
| (330) | Feedwater System Pipe Break | Resolved | (SER)<br>(SSER 14)<br>(SSER 24) | 15.3.3 | |
| (331) | Reactor Coolant Pump Rotor Seizure | Resolved | (SER)<br>(SSER 14)<br>(SSER 24) | 15.3.4 | |
| (332) | Reactor Coolant Pump Shaft Break | Resolved | (SER)<br>(SSER 14)<br>(SSER 24) | 15.3.5 | |
| (333) | Anticipated Transients Without Scram | Resolved | (SER)<br>(SSER 3)<br>(SSER 5)<br>(SSER 6)<br>(SSER 10)<br>(SSER 11)<br>(SSER 12)<br>(SSER 24) | 15.3.6 | |
| (334) | Conclusions | Resolved | (SER) | 15.3.7 | |
| (335) | Radiological Consequences of Accidents | Resolved | (SER)<br>(SSER 15)<br>(SSER 25) | 15.4 | |
| (336) | Loss-of-Coolant Accident | Resolved | (SER)<br>(SSER 5)<br>(SSER 9)<br>(SSER 18)<br>(SSER 25) | 15.4.1 | |
| (337) | Main Steamline Break Outside of Containment | Open (NRR) | (SER)<br>(SSER 15)<br>(SSER 25) | 15.4.2 | |
| (338) | Steam Generator Tube Rupture | Resolved | (SER)<br>(SSER 2)<br>(SSER 5)<br>(SSER 12)<br>(SSER 14)<br>(SSER 15)<br>(SSER 25) | 15.4.3 | |
| (339) | Control Rod Ejection Accident | Resolved | (SER)<br>(SSER 15)<br>(SSER 25) | 15.4.4 | |

| | Issue | Status | | Section | Note |
|---|---|---|---|---|---|
| (340) | Fuel-Handling Accident | Resolved | (SER) (SSER 4) (SSER 15) (SSER 25) | 15.4.5 | |
| (341) | Failure of Small Line Carrying Coolant Outside Containment | Resolved | (SER) (SSER 25) | 15.4.6 | |
| (342) | Postulated Radioactive Releases as a Result of Liquid Tank Failures | Resolved | (SER) (SSER 25) | 15.4.7 | |
| (342a) | Postulated Waste Gas Decay Tank Rupture | Resolved | (SSER 25) | 15.4.8 | |
| (343) | NUREG-0737 Items | | | 15.5 | |
| (344) | Thermal Mechanical Report (TMI Action Item II.K.2.13) | Resolved | (SER) (SSER 4) (SSER 24) | 15.5.1 | |
| (345) | Voiding in the Reactor Coolant System during Transients (TMI Action Item II.K.2.17) | Resolved | (SER) (SSER 4) (SSER 24) | 15.5.2 | |
| (346) | Installation and Testing of Automatic Power-Operated Relief Valve Isolation System (TMI Action Item II.K.3.1) Report on Overall Safety Effect of Power-Operated Relief Valve Isolation System (TMI Action Item II.K.3.2) | Resolved | (SER) (SSER 5) | 15.5.3 | |
| (347) | Automatic Trip of Reactor Coolant Pumps (TMI Action Item II.K.3.5) | Resolved | (SER) (SSER 4) (SSER 16) (SSER 24) | 15.5.4 | |
| (348) | Small-Break LOCA Methods (II.K.3.30) and Plant-Specific Calculations (II.K.3.31) | Open (Inspection) | (SER) (SSER 4) (SSER 5) (SSER 16) | 15.5.5 | |
| (349) | Relative Risk of Low-Power Operation | Resolved | (SER) | 15.6 | |
| (350) | Technical Specification | Open (NRR) | | 16 | |
| (351) | Quality Assurance | | | 17 | |
| (352) | General | Resolved | (SER) | 17.1 | |
| (353) | Organization | Resolved | (SER) | 17.2 | |
| (354) | Quality Assurance Program | Resolved | (SER) (SSER 2) (SSER 5) (SSER 10) (SSER 13) (SSER 15) (SSER 22) | 17.3 | |
| (355) | Conclusions | Resolved | (SER) | 17.4 | |
| (356) | Maintenance Rule | | | 17.6 | |
| (357) | Control Room Design Review | | | 18 | |

| | Issue | Status | | Section | Note |
|---|---|---|---|---|---|
| (358) | General | Resolved | (SER) (SSER 5) (SSER 6) (SSER 15) (SSER 16) (SSER 22) | 18.1 | |
| (359) | Conclusions | Resolved | (SER) (SSER 16) (SSER 22) | 18.2 | |
| (360) | Report of the Advisory Committee on Reactor Safeguards | | (SER) | 19 | |
| (361) | Common Defense and Security | | (SER) | 20 | |
| (362) | Financial Qualifications | | (SER) | 21 | |
| (363) | TVA Financial Qualifications for WBN Unit 2 | | (SSER 22) (SSER 23) | 21.1 | |
| (364) | Foreign Ownership, Control, or Domination | | (SSER 22) | 21.2 | |
| (365) | Financial Protection and Indemnity Requirements | | | 22 | |
| (366) | General | | (SER) | 22.1 | |
| (367) | Preoperational Storage of Nuclear Fuel | | (SER) | 22.2 | |
| (368) | Operating Licenses | Open (NRR) | (SSER 22) | 22.3 | |
| (369) | Quality of Construction, Operational Readiness, and Quality Assurance Effectiveness | | | 25 | |
| (370) | Program for Maintenance and Preservation of the Licensing Basis for Units 1 and 2 | Open (NRR) | (SSER 22) | 25.9 | |

Notes:

1.  In the process of further validating the information in the WBN Unit 2 FSAR, TVA identified minor administrative/typographical changes to sections previously considered Resolved. TVA addressed these changes to the applicable sections in their submittals and clearly indicated them to the staff. The staff has reviewed and confirmed that the changes made are administrative/typographical and do not impact the staff's conclusions as stated in previous SSERs. Based on this review, no additional review is necessary and this section remains Resolved.

2.  During the assessment of the regulatory framework for completion of the project, the staff characterized certain topics as "Open" pending TVA's validation of the information contained in the section. TVA has determined that the information presented in the FSAR remained valid and only identified minor administrative or typographical changes to the section. TVA addressed the changes in their submittals and clearly indicated the changes. The staff reviewed and confirmed that the changes made to the section are administrative/typographical and do not impact its conclusions as stated in previous SSERs. Therefore, no additional review is necessary and the staff considers this section Resolved.

3. In SSER 21, this issue was identified as "Resolved." However, TVA made changes to the Unit 2 FSAR affecting the previous staff conclusions. The staff evaluated the changes and the results are documented in this SSER.

## 1.8 Confirmatory Issues

At this point in the review, there are some items that have essentially been resolved to the staff's satisfaction, but for which certain confirmatory information has not yet been provided by the applicant. In these instances, the applicant has committed to provide the confirmatory information in the near future. If staff review of this information does not confirm preliminary conclusions on an item, that item will be treated as open, and the NRC staff will report on its resolution in a supplement to this report.

The confirmatory items, with appropriate references to subsections of this report, are noted in Appendix HH.

## 1.9 License Conditions

The NRC staff proposes two license conditions discussed in Section 2.4.10 of SSER 24.

**Flooding Protection Proposed License Condition No. 1:**

TVA will submit to the NRC staff by August 31, 2012, for review and approval, a summary of the results of the finite element analysis, which demonstrates that the Cherokee and Douglas dams are fully stable under design basis probable maximum flood loading conditions for the long-term stability analysis, including how the preestablished acceptance criteria were met.

**Flooding Protection Proposed License Condition No. 2:**

TVA will submit to the NRC staff, before completion of the first operating cycle, its long-term modification plan to raise the height of the embankments associated with the Cherokee, Fort Loudoun, Tellico, and Watts Bar dams. The submittal shall include analyses to demonstrate that, when the modifications are complete, the embankments will meet the applicable structural loading conditions, stability requirements, and functionality considerations to ensure that the design basis probable maximum flood limits are not exceeded at the Watts Bar Nuclear Plant. All modifications to raise the height of the embankments shall be completed within 3 years from the date of issuance of the operating license.

The NRC staff proposes two license conditions discussed in Section 13.6.6.3.22 of SSER 24.

**Cyber Security Proposed License Condition 1:**

The licensee shall implement the requirements of 10 CFR 73.54(a)(1)(ii) as they relate to the security computer. Completion of these actions will occur consistent with the full implementation date of September 30, 2014, as established in the licensee's letter dated April 7, 2011, "Response to Request for Additional Information Regarding Watts Bar Nuclear Plant Cyber Security Plan License Amendment Request, Cyber Security Plan Implementation Schedule - Watts Bar Nuclear Plant Unit 1."

**Cyber Security Proposed License Condition 2:**

> The licensee shall implement the requirements of 10 CFR 73.54(a)(1)(iii) as they relate to the corporate based systems that support emergency preparedness. Completion of these actions will occur consistent with the Watts Bar Nuclear Plant Unit 1 implementation schedule established in the licensee's letter dated April 7, 2011, "Response to Request for Additional Information Regarding Watts Bar Nuclear Plant Cyber Security Plan License Amendment Request, Cyber Security Plan Implementation Schedule - Watts Bar Nuclear Plant Unit 1."

## 1.10 Unresolved Safety Issues

Section 210 of the Energy Reorganization Act of 1974, as amended, states, in part,

> The Commission shall develop a plan for providing for specification and analysis of unresolved safety issues relating to nuclear reactors and shall take such action as may be necessary to implement corrective measures with respect to such issues.

The NRC staff continuously evaluates the safety requirements used in its review against new information as it becomes available. In some cases, the staff takes immediate action or interim measures to ensure safety. In most cases, however, the initial assessment indicates that immediate licensing actions or changes in licensing criteria are not necessary. In any event, further study may be deemed appropriate to make judgments as to whether existing requirements should be modified. The issues being studied are sometimes called generic safety issues because they are related to a particular class or type of nuclear facility.

The NRC staff documented its original review of Unresolved Safety Issues for WBN Units 1 and 2 in Appendix C to the safety evaluation report (SER; NUREG-0847, June 1982). A discussion of the status of resolution of these generic issues for TVA's application for an operating license for WBN Unit 2 is provided in Appendix C to SSER 23, dated July 2011.

## 1.13 Implementation of Corrective Action Programs and Special Programs

In 1985, TVA developed a corporate Nuclear Performance Plan (NPP) that identified and proposed corrections to problems concerning the overall management of its nuclear program and a site-specific plan for WBN entitled, "Watts Bar Nuclear Performance Plan." TVA established 18 corrective action programs (CAPs) and 11 special programs (SPs) to address these concerns.

SSER 21, Table 1.13.1 documented the status of staff review of the CAPs and SPs. This SSER and future supplements to the SER, the staff will document its evaluation and closure of open NPP items.

## 1.13.1 Corrective Action Programs

| No. | Title | Program Review Status |
|-----|-------|----------------------|
| (1) | Cable Issues<br>a.  Silicon Rubber Insulated Cable<br>b.  Cable Jamming<br>c.  Cable Support in Vertical Conduit<br>d.  Cable Support in Vertical Trays<br>e.  Cable Proximity to Hot Pipes<br>f.  Cable Pull-Bys<br>g.  Cable Bend Radius<br>h.  Cable Splices<br>i.  Cable Sidewall Bearing Pressure<br>j.  Pulling Cables Through 90° Condulet and Flexible Conduit<br>k.  Computer Cable Routing System Software and Database Verification and Validation | Resolved<br>(See Appendix HH) |
| (2) | Cable Tray and Tray Supports | Resolved |
| (3) | Design Baseline and Verification Program | Resolved |
| (4) | Electrical Conduit and Conduit Support | Resolved |
| (5) | Electrical Issues<br>a.  Flexible Conduit Installations<br>b.  Physical Cable Separation and Electrical Isolation<br>c.  Contact and Coil Rating of Electrical Devices<br>d.  Torque Switch and Overload Relay Bypass Capability for Active Safety-Related Valves<br>e.  Adhesive-Backed Cable Support Mount | Resolved<br>(See Appendix HH) |
| (6) | Equipment Seismic Qualification | Resolved |
| (7) | Fire protection | Resolved |
| (8) | Hanger and Analysis Update Program | Resolved |
| (9) | Heat Code Traceability | Resolved |
| (10) | Heating, Ventilation, and Air-Conditioning Duct and Duct Supports | Resolved |
| (11) | Instrument Lines | Resolved |
| (12) | Prestart Test Program Plan | Resolved |
| (13) | Quality Assurance (QA) Records | Resolved |
| (14) | Quality-List (Q-List) | Resolved |

| No. | Title | Program Review Status |
|-----|-------|----------------------|
| (15) | Replacement Items Program (Piece Parts) | Resolved |
| (16) | Seismic Analysis | Resolved |
| (17) | Vendor Information Program | Resolved |
| (18) | Welding | Resolved |

## 1.13.2 Special Programs

| No. | Title | Program Review Status |
|-----|-------|----------------------|
| (1) | Concrete Quality Program | Resolved |
| (2) | Containment Cooling | Resolved |
| (3) | Detailed Control Room Design Review | Resolved |
| (4) | Environmental Qualifications Program | Resolved |
| (5) | Master Fuse List | Resolved |
| (6) | Mechanical Equipment Qualification | Resolved |
| (7) | Microbiologically Induced Corrosion | Resolved |
| (8) | Moderate Energy Line Break Flooding | Resolved |
| (9) | Radiation Monitoring System | Resolved |
| (11) | Use-As-Is Condition Adverse to Quality | Resolved |

## 1.14   Implementation of Applicable Bulletin and Generic Letter Requirements

From time to time, the NRC staff issues generic requirements or recommendations in the form of orders, bulletins (BLs), generic letters (GLs), regulatory issue summaries, and other documents to address certain safety and regulatory issues. These are generally termed "generic communications."

The table below outlines the status of the resolution of the generic communications identified in SSER 21. It should be noted that, although many of the generic communications have been documented or otherwise resolved, the NRC staff has determined that there may be circumstances that could result in the need to reopen a previously closed topic.

|  | Correspondence No. | Title |
|---|---|---|
| (1) | GL 1980-14 | Light-Water Reactor Primary Coolant System Pressure Isolation Valves. |
|  | TVA Action: | Submit Technical Specifications (TSs) for NRC Review. |
|  | NRC Action: | To be reviewed during validation of TS 3.4.14 submitted February 2, 2010. |
| (2) | GL 1980-77 | Refueling Water Level - Technical Specifications Changes. |
|  | TVA Action: | Submit Technical Specifications for NRC Review. |
|  | NRC Action: | To be reviewed during validation of TS 3.9.5 –TS 3.9.7 submitted February 2, 2010. |
| (3) | GL 1982-28 | Inadequate Core Cooling Instrumentation System. |
|  | TVA Action: | Closed. |
|  | NRC Action: | Closed. Subsumed as part of NRC staff review of Instrumentation and Controls submitted April 8, 2010. |
| (4) | GL 1983-28 | Required Actions Based on Generic Implications of Salem Anticipated Transient without Scram Events (Screened into the Items 4 through 7). |
| (4.a) | GL 1983-28 (item 3.1) | Post-Maintenance Testing (reactor trip system components). |
|  |  | Submit Technical Specifications for NRC Review. |
|  | TVA Action: |  |
|  |  | To be reviewed during validation of TS Bases 3.0.1 submitted |
|  | NRC Action: | March 4, 2009. |

| | Correspondence No. | Title |
|---|---|---|
| (4.b) | GL 1983-28 (3.2) | Post-Maintenance Testing (All Surveillance Requirement Components). |
| | TVA Action | Submit Technical Specifications and NRC Review. |
| | NRC Action | To be reviewed during validation of TS Bases 3.0.1 submitted March 4, 2009. |
| (4.c) | GL 1983-28 (4.2) | Reactor Trip System Reliability (Preventive Maintenance and Surveillance Program for Reactor Trip Breakers). |
| | TVA Action | Submit Technical Specifications and NRC Review. |
| | NRC Action | To be reviewed during staff evaluation of Item 17 of TS Table 3.3.1-1 submitted February 2, 2010. |
| (4.d) | GL 1983-28 (4.5) | Reactor Trip System Reliability (Automatic Actuation of Shunt Trip Attachment). |
| | TVA Action | Submit Technical Specifications and NRC Review. |
| | NRC Action | To be reviewed during staff evaluation of Item 18 of TS Table 3.3.1-1 submitted February 2, 2010. |
| (8) | GL 1986-09 | Technical Resolution of Generic Issue B-59, (N-1) Loop Operation in BWRs and PWRs. |
| | TVA Action | Submit Technical Specifications for NRC Review. |
| | NRC Action | To be reviewed during validation of TS 3.4.4 - TS 3.4.8 submitted February 2, 2010. |
| (9) | GL 1988-20 | Individual Plant Examination for Severe Accident Vulnerability. |
| | TVA Action | Closed. |
| | NRC Action | Closed. NRC letter dated August 12, 2011 (ADAMS Accession No. ML111960228). |
| (10) | GL 1988-20s1 | Initiation of the Individual Plant Examination for Severe Accident Vulnerabilities — 10 CFR 50.54. |
| | TVA Action | Closed. |
| | NRC Action | Closed. NRC letter dated August 12, 2011 (ADAMS Accession No. ML111960228). |

| Correspondence No. | Title |
|---|---|
| (11) GL 1988-20s2 | Individual Plant Examination for Severe Accident Vulnerability. Accident Management Strategies for Consideration in the Individual Plant Examination Process. |
| TVA Action | Closed. |
| NRC Action | Closed. NRC letter dated August 12, 2011 (ADAMS Accession No. ML111960228). |
| (12) GL 1988-20s3 | Individual Plant Examination for Severe Accident Vulnerability. Completion of Containment Performance Improvement Program and Forwarding of Insights for Use in the IPE for Severe Accident Vulnerabilities. |
| TVA Action | Closed. |
| NRC Action | Closed. NRC letter dated August 12, 2011 (ADAMS Accession No. ML111960228). |
| (13) GL 1988-20s4 | Individual Plant Examination of External Events (IPEEE) for Severe Accident Vulnerabilities. |
| TVA Action | Closed. |
| NRC Action | Closed. NRC letter dated September 20, 2011 (ADAMS Accession No. ML111960300). |
| (14) GL 1988-20s5 | Individual Plant Examination of External Events (IPEEE) for Severe Accident Vulnerabilities - 10 CFR 50.54(f). |
| TVA Action | Closed. |
| NRC Action | Closed. NRC letter dated September 20, 2011 (ADAMS Accession No. ML111960300). |
| (15) GL 1989-04 | Guidelines on Developing Acceptable Inservice Testing Programs. |
| TVA Action | The proposed approach has been approved for WBN Unit 1; the same approach will be proposed for use on WBN Unit 2 without change. |
| NRC Action | Open. |

| Correspondence No. | Title |
|---|---|
| (16) GL 1989-21 | Request for Information Concerning Status of Implementation of Unresolved Safety Issue Requirements. |
| TVA Action | TVA provided an updated status of unresolved safety issues on September 26, 2008, as supplemented on December 2, 2010, and January 25, 2011. |
| NRC Action | Closed. See Appendix C of SSER 23. |
| (17) GL 1990-06 | Resolution of Generic Issues 70, "PORV [power-operated relief valve] and Block Valve Reliability," and 94, "Additional LTOP [low-temperature overpressure] Protection for PWRs." |
| TVA Action | Submit Technical Specifications for NRC Review. |
| NRC Action | To be reviewed during validation of TS 3.4.11 - TS 3.4.12 submitted February 2, 2010. |
| (18) GL 1992-08 | Thermo-Lag 330-1 Fire Barriers. |
| TVA Action | The proposed approach has been approved for WBN Unit 1; the same approach will be proposed for use on WBN Unit 2 without change. |
| NRC Action | Open. Pending NRC staff inspection verification. |
| (19) GL 1995-03 | Circumferential cracking of Steam Generator (SG) Tubes. |
| TVA Action | The proposed approach has been approved for WBN Unit 1; the same approach was submitted for use on WBN Unit 2 without change. |
| NRC Action | Closed. NRC Letter dated January 21, 2010 (ADAMS Accession No. ML093631061). |
| (20) GL 1995-05 | Voltage –Based Repair Criteria for Westinghouse Steam Generator Tubes affected by Outside Diameter Stress Corrosion Cracking. |
| TVA Action | The proposed approach has been approved for WBN Unit 1; the same approach was submitted for use on WBN Unit 2 without change. |
| NRC Action | Closed. NRC Letter dated January 21, 2010 (ADAMS Accession No. ML093631061). |

| Correspondence No. | Title |
|---|---|
| (21) GL 1996-06 | Assurance of Equipment Operability and Containment Integrity During Design-Basis Accident Conditions. |
| TVA Action | The proposed approach has been approved for WBN Unit 1; the same approach will be proposed for use on WBN Unit 2 without change. |
| NRC Action | Closed. NRC Letter dated January 21, 2010 (ADAMS Accession No. ML100130227). |
| (22) GL 1995-07 | Pressure Locking and Thermal Binding of Safety-Related Power-Operated Gate Valves (Not identified in SSER 21 as "Open"). |
| TVA Action | The proposed approach has been approved for WBN Unit 1; the same approach will be proposed for use on WBN Unit 2 without change. |
| NRC Action | Closed. NRC letter dated August 12, 2010 (ADAMS Accession No. ML100190443). |
| (23) GL 1997-01 | Degradation of Control Rod Drive Mechanism Nozzle and Other Vessel Closure Head Penetrations. |
| TVA Action | The proposed approach has been approved for WBN Unit 1; the same approach will be proposed for use on WBN Unit 2 without change. |
| NRC Action | Closed. NRC Letter dated June 30, 2010 (ADAMS Accession No. ML100539515). |
| (24) GL 1997-04 | Assurance of Sufficient Net Positive Suction Head for Emergency Core Cooling and Containment Heat Removal Pumps Integrity During Design-Basis Accident Conditions. |
| TVA Action | The proposed approach has been approved for WBN Unit 1; the same approach was submitted for use on WBN Unit 2 without change. |
| NRC Action | Closed. NRC Letter dated February 18, 2010 (ADAMS Accession No. ML100200375). |

| Correspondence No. | Title |
|---|---|
| (25) | GL 1997-05 | SG Tube Inspection Techniques. |

**(25)  GL 1997-05**   SG Tube Inspection Techniques.

TVA Action   The proposed approach has been approved for WBN Unit 1; the same approach was submitted for use on WBN Unit 2 without change.

NRC Action   Closed. NRC Letter dated January 21, 2010 (ADAMS Accession No. ML093631061).

**(26)  GL 1997-06**   Degradation of SG Internals.

TVA Action   The proposed approach has been approved for WBN Unit 1; the same approach was submitted for use on WBN Unit 2 without change.

NRC Action   Closed. NRC Letter dated January 21, 2010 (ADAMS Accession No. ML093631061).

**(27)  GL 1998-02**   Loss of Reactor Coolant Inventory and Associated Potential for Loss of Emergency Mitigation Functions While in a Shutdown Condition.

TVA Action   The proposed approach has been approved for WBN Unit 1; the same approach will be proposed for use on WBN Unit 2 without change.

NRC Action   Closed. NRC Letter dated May 11, 2010 (ADAMS Accession No. ML101200155).

**(28)  GL 1998-04**   Potential for Degradation of the ECCS [Emergency Core Cooling System] and the Containment Spray System after a LOCA because of Construction and Protective Coating Deficiencies and Foreign Material in Containment.

TVA Action   The proposed approach has been approved for WBN Unit 1; the same approach was submitted for use on WBN Unit 2 without change.

NRC Action   Closed. NRC Letter dated February 1, 2010 (ADAMS Accession No. ML100260594).

| Correspondence No. | Title |
|---|---|
| (29) GL 2003-01 | Control Room Habitability. |
| TVA Action | No action or documentation is provided to show the staff has reviewed the item for WBN Unit 2, and the resolution is through submittal of a technical specification. |
| NRC Action | Closed. NRC Letter dated February 1, 2010 (ADAMS Accession No. ML100270076). |
| (30) GL 2004-01 | Requirements for SG Tube Inspection. |
| TVA Action | The proposed approach has been approved for WBN Unit 1; the same approach was submitted for use on WBN Unit 2 without change. |
| NRC Action | Closed. NRC Letter dated January 21, 2010 (ADAMS Accession No. ML093631061). |
| (31) GL 2004-02 | Potential Impact of Debris Blockage on Emergency Recirculation during Design-Basis Accidents at PWRs. |
| TVA Action | The proposed approach has been approved for WBN Unit 1; the same approach was submitted for use on WBN Unit 2 without change. |
| NRC Action | Open. |
| (32) GL 2006-01 | SG Tube Integrity and Associated Technical Specifications. |
| TVA Action | No action or documentation is provided to show the staff has reviewed the item for WBN Unit 2, and the resolution is through submittal of a technical specification. |
| NRC Action | Closed. NRC Letter dated January 21, 2010 (ADAMS Accession No. ML093631061) (See Appendix HH). |
| (33) GL 2006-02 | Grid Reliability and the Impact on Plant Risk and the Operability of Offsite Power. |
| TVA Action | The proposed approach has been approved for WBN Unit 1; the same approach was submitted for use on WBN Unit 2 without change. |
| NRC Action | Closed. NRC Letter dated January 21, 2010 (ADAMS Accession No. ML093631061) (See Appendix HH). |

| Correspondence No. | Title |
|---|---|

**(34)** GL 2006-03 — Potentially Nonconforming Hemyc and MT Fire Barrier Configurations.

TVA Action — The proposed approach has been approved for WBN Unit 1; the same approach was submitted for use on WBN Unit 2 without change.

NRC Action — Closed. NRC Letter February 25, 2010 (ADAMS Accession No. ML100470398).

**(35)** GL 2007-01 — Inaccessible or Underground Power Cable Failures that Disable Accident Mitigation Systems or Cause Plant Transients.

TVA Action — The proposed approach has been approved for WBN Unit 1; the same approach was submitted for use on WBN Unit 2 without change.

NRC Action — Closed. NRC Letter dated January 26, 2010 (ADAMS Accession No. ML100120052).

**(36)** GL 2008-01 — Managing Gas Accumulation in Emergency Core Cooling, Decay Heat Removal, and Containment Spray Systems.

TVA Action — TVA submitted the information requested by the GL.

NRC Action — Closed. NRC letter dated August 23, 2011 (ADAMS Accession No. ML112232205).

**(37)** BL 1992-01 and Supplement 1 — Failure of Thermo-Lag 330 Fire Barrier System to Perform its Specified Fire Endurance Function.

TVA Action — The proposed approach has been approved for WBN Unit 1; the same approach will be proposed for use on WBN Unit 2 without change.

NRC Action — Open. Pending NRC staff inspection verification.

**(38)** BL 1996-01 — Control Rod Insertion Problems (PWR)

TVA Action — The proposed approach has been approved for WBN Unit 1; the same approach was submitted for use on WBN Unit 2 without change.

NRC Action — Closed. NRC letter dated May 3, 2010 (ADAMS Accession No. ML101200035) required Confirmatory Action (See Appendix HH).

| Correspondence No. | Title |
|---|---|

(39)    BL 1996-02      Movement of Heavy Loads Over Spent Fuel, Over Fuel In the Reactor Core, or Over Safety-Related Equipment.

The proposed approach has been approved for WBN Unit 1; the same approach was submitted for use on WBN Unit 2 without change.

Closed. NRC Letter dated March 4, 2010 (ADAMS Accession No. ML100480062).

(40)    BL 2001-01      Circumferential Cracking of Reactor Pressure Vessel (RPV) Head Penetration Nozzles.

TVA Action      The proposed approach has been approved for WBN Unit 1; the same approach was submitted for use on WBN Unit 2 without change.

NRC Action      Closed. See NRC Letter dated June 30, 2010 (ADAMS Accession No. ML 100539515).

(41)    BL 2002-01      RPV Head Degradation and Reactor Coolant Pressure Boundary Integrity.

TVA Action      The proposed approach has been approved for WBN Unit 1; the same approach was submitted for use on WBN Unit 2 without change.

NRC Action      Closed. See NRC Letter dated June 30, 2010 (ADAMS Accession No. ML 100539515).

(42)    BL 2002-02      RPV Head and Vessel Head Penetration Nozzle Inspection Program.

TVA Action      The proposed approach has been approved for WBN Unit 1; the same approach was submitted for use on WBN Unit 2 without change.

NRC Action      Closed. See NRC Letter dated June 30, 2010 (ADAMS Accession No. ML100539515).

|  | Correspondence No. | Title |
|---|---|---|
| (43) | BL 2003-02 | Leakage from RPV Lower Head Penetrations and Reactor Coolant Pressure Boundary Integrity. |
|  | TVA Action | The proposed approach has been approved for WBN Unit 1; the same approach was submitted for use on WBN Unit 2 without change. |
|  | NRC Action | Closed. NRC Letter dated January 21, 2010 (ADAMS Accession No. ML093631061). |
| (44) | BL 2004-01 | Inspection of Alloy 82/182/600 Materials Used in the Fabrication of Pressurizer Penetrations and Steam Space Piping Connections at PWRs. |
|  | TVA Action | The proposed approach has been approved for WBN Unit 1; the same approach was submitted for use on WBN Unit 2 without change. |
|  | NRC Action | Closed. NRC letter dated August 4, 2010 (ADAMS Accession No. ML102080017). |
| (45) | BL 2007-01 | Security Officer Attentiveness. |
|  | TVA Action | The proposed approach has been approved for WBN Unit 1; the same approach will be proposed for use on WBN Unit 2 without change. |
|  | NRC Action | Closed. NRC letter dated March 25, 2010 (ADAMS Accession No. ML100770549). |

NUREG-0737, TMI Action Items (TVA letter dated September 14, 1981, applies to all of the following NUREG-0737 issues):

|  | Correspondence No. | Title |
|---|---|---|
| (46) | NUREG-0737 Item I.B.1.2 | Independent Safety Engineering Group. |
|  | TVA Action | The proposed approach has been approved for WBN Unit 1; the same approach will be proposed for use on WBN Unit 2 without change. |
|  | NRC Action | Open. |

| Correspondence No. | Title |
|---|---|

(47)    NUREG-0737      Control Room Design Review (CRDR).
Item I.D.1

          TVA Action      The proposed approach has been approved for WBN Unit 1; the same approach will be proposed for use on WBN Unit 2 without change.

          NRC Action      Closed in SSER 22, Section 18.2.

(48)    NUREG-0737      Post-accident Sampling.
Item II.B.3

          TVA Action      No action or documentation is provided to show the staff has reviewed the item for WBN Unit 2, and the resolution is through submittal of a technical specification.

          NRC Action      Closed in SSER 24, Section 9.3.2.

(49)    NUREG-0737      Containment Isolation Dependability.
Item II.E.4.2

          TVA Action      No action or documentation is provided to show the staff has reviewed the item for WBN Unit 2, and the resolution is through submittal of a technical specification.

          NRC Action      Open.

(50)    NUREG-0737      Instrumentation for Detection of Inadequate Core-Cooling.
Item II.F.2

          TVA Action      Open.

          NRC Action      Open. See SSER 23, Section 4.4.8.

(51)    NUREG-0737      Reporting SV/RV Failures/Challenges.
Item II.K.3.3

          TVA Action      No action or documentation is provided to show the staff has reviewed the item for WBN Unit 2, and the resolution is through submittal of a technical specification.

          NRC Action      Closed in SSER 22, Section 13.5.3.

| Correspondence No. | Title |
|---|---|

(52)      NUREG-0737         Anticipatory Trip at High Power.
Item II.K.3.10

         TVA Action           No action or documentation is provided to show the staff has reviewed the item for WBN Unit 2, and the resolution is through submittal of a technical specification.

         NRC Action           Open.

(53)      NUREG-0737         Primary Coolant Outside Containment.
Item III.D.1.1

         TVA Action           No action or documentation is provided to show the staff has reviewed the item for WBN Unit 2, and the resolution is through submittal of a technical specification.

         NRC Action           Open.

(54)      NUREG-0737         Control-Room Habitability.
Item III.D.3.4

         TVA Action           The proposed approach has been approved for WBN Unit 1; the same approach will be proposed for use on WBN Unit 2 without change.

         NRC Action           Closed in SSER 22, Section 6.4.

(55)      IEB 75-08           PWR Pressure Instrumentation.

         TVA Action           The item has been approved either for both units at WBN or explicitly for WBN Unit 2; however, a change to the original approval requires submittal of the technical specifications and staff review.

         NRC Action           Open.

(56)      IEB 77-04           Calculation Error Affecting Performance of a System for Controlling pH of Containment Sump Water Following a LOCA.

         TVA Action           The item has been approved either for both units at WBN or explicitly for WBN Unit 2; however, a change to the original approval requires submittal of the technical specifications and staff review.

         NRC Action

         Open.

2      SITE CHARACTERISTICS

2.3    Meteorology

2.3.3   Onsite Meteorological Measurements Program

The U.S. Nuclear Regulatory Commission (NRC) guidance provided in NUREG-0800, "Standard Review Plan for the Review of Safety Analysis Reports for Nuclear Power Plants: LWR Edition" (SRP), Section 2.3.3, "Onsite Meteorological Measurements Programs," Revision 2, issued July 1981, states, in part, that when the final safety analysis report (FSAR) is docketed, an applicant should provide at least two consecutive annual cycles, including the most recent 1-year period, of onsite meteorological measurements. The applicant should summarize the data to describe the meteorological characteristics of the site and its vicinity in formats suitable for making atmospheric dispersion estimates for both postulated accidental and expected routine airborne releases of effluents. In addition, the applicant should provide evidence of how well the data represent long-term conditions at the site.

To meet these objectives, the Tennessee Valley Authority (TVA) provided the following sets of meteorological data for the Watts Bar Nuclear Plant (WBN):

- hourly data from 1991 through 2010 formatted to calculate short-term design-basis accident (DBA) control room (CR) atmospheric dispersion estimates ($\chi/Q$ values) using the ARCON96 atmospheric dispersion computer code (NUREG/CR-6331, "Atmospheric Relative Concentrations in Building Wakes," Revision 1, issued 1996), provided by letter dated October 17, 2011 (Agencywide Documents Access and Management System (ADAMS) Accession No. ML11294A461)

- a joint frequency distribution (JFD) of wind speed and direction by atmospheric stability class of the data from 1991 through 2010, provided by letter dated November 7, 2011, to calculate the DBA exclusion area boundary (EAB) and low-population zone (LPZ) $\chi/Q$ values

- a JFD of data from 1986 through 2005 provided in FSAR Amendment 105, dated August 12, 2011 (ADAMS Accession No. ML11236A158), to calculate long-term routine release $\chi/Q$ values and deposition factors (D/Q values)

These data supplemented the JFD information from 1974 through 1993 in the WBN FSAR, previously discussed in Supplemental Safety Evaluation Report (SSER) 15, dated June 15, 1995 (ADAMS Accession No. ML072060488).

The NRC staff reviewed the onsite hourly meteorological data for 1991 through 2010 using the methodology described in NUREG-0917, "NRC Staff Computer Programs for Use with Meteorological Data," issued July 1982. Further statistical review used computer spreadsheets. Data recovery for the 20-year period for all parameters was consistently in the upper 90 percentiles, which exceeds the recommendation of NRC Regulatory Guide (RG) 1.23, "Onsite Meteorological Programs," issued June 1972, of at least 90-percent data recovery. With respect to atmospheric stability measurements, stable and neutral conditions were consistently reported to occur at night, and unstable and neutral conditions occurred during the day. The frequency, length, and time of occurrence of stable and unstable atmospheric conditions were congruent with expected meteorological conditions. Wind speed and direction frequency distributions for each measurement channel were also very consistent from year to year and when comparing measurements between the measurement heights. Meteorological data summarized in the JFD formats were reasonably consistent with the data provided in the hourly data summary formats. On the basis of this review, the NRC staff concluded that the data files provided by TVA for 1991 through 2010 give an adequate representation of the site conditions to facilitate calculation of the CR, EAB, and LPZ $\chi/Q$ values for DBA and $\chi/Q$ and $D/Q$ values for routine release dose assessments for WBN Unit 2.

The JFD summary for the data from 1991 through 2010 provided by letter dated November 7, 2011, and a discussion of the long-term representativeness of these data should be provided in the WBN Unit 2 FSAR. Upon receipt of the updated FSAR, the NRC staff will confirm that these updates have been made by TVA. This is **Open Item 136** (Appendix HH).

2.3.4  Short-Term (Accident) Atmospheric Dispersion Estimates

As discussed in its letter dated July 31, 2010 (ADAMS Accession No. ML102290258), TVA initially based the WBN Unit 2 DBA $\chi/Q$ values for the CR, EAB, and LPZ on meteorological data from 1974 through 1993, which were used as the licensing basis for WBN Unit 1. TVA subsequently compared these data with current meteorological conditions and concluded that it was appropriate to update the WBN Unit 2 DBA $\chi/Q$ values for the CR, EAB, and LPZ to incorporate more recent meteorological data using the 20-year period from 1991 through 2010.

TVA used the ARCON96 methodology to calculate the WBN Unit 2 CR $\chi/Q$ values using inputs and assumptions initially discussed in Enclosure 1 and Attachments 11 and 12 to its letter dated July 31, 2010. TVA stated that it based the dose analysis and associated release scenarios on NRC guidance documentation and considered worst case single failures. The applicant assumed loss of offsite power (LOOP) for all accidents, in addition to the worst case single failure. It modeled all releases as ground-level point sources using the straight-line horizontal distance as the distance of separation between each postulated source and receptor pair. No sources were modeled as diffuse or high-energy releases. Following completion of further analyses, TVA provided a supplemental letter dated September 15, 2011 (ADAMS Accession No. ML11262A276), which summarized the revised $\chi/Q$ values used in the dose assessments for the loss-of-coolant, fuel-handling, steam generator tube rupture, main steamline break, and loss of alternating current power accidents.

RG 1.194, "Atmospheric Relative Concentrations for Control Room Radiological Habitability Assessments at Nuclear Power Plants," issued June 2003, states that ARCON96 is an acceptable methodology for assessing CR $\chi/Q$ values for use in DBA radiological analyses. The NRC staff evaluated the applicability of the ARCON96 model and concluded that no unusual siting, building arrangement, release characterization, source-receptor configuration, meteorological regime, or terrain conditions precluded use of this model in support of the WBN Unit 2 license application. The NRC staff qualitatively reviewed TVA's inputs to the ARCON96 computer runs and found them adequately consistent with site configuration drawings and staff practice. The NRC staff noted that TVA used the ARCON96 default constant values for surface roughness length and averaging sector width presented in NUREG/CR-6331, Revision 1, rather than the default values listed in RG 1.194. The NRC staff used ARCON96 and the RG 1.194 default values to calculate $\chi/Q$ values to compare with the $\chi/Q$ values calculated by TVA. The staff concluded that the CR $\chi/Q$ values identified in TVA's letter dated September 15, 2011, are acceptable for use in the DBA dose assessment associated with the WBN Unit 2 license application, because the $\chi/Q$ values calculated by TVA were either similar to, or bounding for, the ARCON96 and the RG 1.194 default values.

By letter dated June 27, 2011 (ADAMS Accession No. ML11180A280), TVA provided updated EAB and LPZ χ/Q values and information related to development of the updated values that it generated using the meteorological data from 1991 through 2010. TVA stated that it based the updated χ/Q values on guidance in RG 1.145, "Atmospheric Dispersion Models for Potential Accident Consequence Assessments at Nuclear Power Plants," and assumed all releases were ground level with a minimum EAB distance of 1,100 meters and LPZ distance of 4,828 meters, which were the same bases as for WBN Unit 1.

The NRC staff qualitatively reviewed the inputs and assumptions used by TVA and found them reasonably consistent with NRC regulatory guidance and staff practice. In addition, the NRC staff made comparison calculations using the PAVAN computer code (NUREG/CR-2858, "PAVAN: An Atmospheric Dispersion Program for Evaluating Design Basis Accidental Releases of Radioactive Material from Nuclear Power Stations," issued 1982) and obtained results similar to the EAB and LPZ χ/Q values generated by TVA.

On the basis of this review, the NRC staff concluded that the CR, EAB, and LPZ χ/Q values are acceptable for use in the WBN Unit 2 DBA dose assessments. Section 15.4, "Radiological Consequences of Accidents," of this SSER discusses the updated CR, EAB, and LPZ χ/Q values with their associated DBA dose assessments.

In its letter dated September 15, 2011, TVA stated that it would revise FSAR Section 15.5 in a future amendment to reflect the χ/Q values presented in that letter. TVA reflected the EAB and LPZ χ/Q values from its letter dated June 27, 2011, in FSAR Amendment 105, dated August 12, 2011 (ADAMS Accession No. ML11236A158). The NRC staff will confirm, upon receipt, that TVA integrated the updated CR χ/Q values from its letter dated September 15, 2011, into a future amendment of the FSAR. This is **Open Item 137** (Appendix HH).

2.3.5  Long-Term (Routine) Atmospheric Dispersion Estimates

SRP Section 2.3.5, "Long-Term Diffusion Estimates," Revision 2, issued July 1981, states that annual average χ/Q and D/Q values should be calculated for specific receptor locations (e.g., site boundary, residence, garden, cow) and for 16 radial sectors, with each radial sector divided into 10 sections, from the site boundary to a distance of 50 miles from the plant, using meteorological data representative of the annual average meteorological characteristics in the vicinity of the plant. Annual average χ/Q and D/Q values are used in the dose assessment associated with the projected routine release of effluents from the plant.

To meet this objective, TVA made the following modifications in the FSAR:

- updated the annual average χ/Q and D/Q values for the WBN specific receptor locations, based upon the meteorology data for 1986 through 2005, and dose receptor and pathway information indicated in the 2007 land use survey

- provided the annual average χ/Q and D/Q values for the 16 radial sectors, based on the data for 1986 through 2005

The updated annual average χ/Q and D/Q values associated with the specific receptor locations appear in Table 11.3-8, and the sets of values for the 16 radial sectors are in Tables 2.3-75A and 2.3-75B, of FSAR Amendment 104, dated June 3, 2011 (ADAMS Accession No. ML11178A155). In addition, in FSAR Section 2.3.5, TVA stated that it discussed this topic in the WBN Offsite Dose Calculation Manual (ODCM). FSAR Section 11.3 also discusses this topic. Upon receipt of the updated ODCM, the NRC staff will confirm that TVA made the corresponding revisions related to the updated annual average $\chi/Q$ and $D/Q$ values. This is **Open Item 138** (Appendix HH).

The NRC staff's review and conclusions regarding the changes proposed by TVA are discussed in Sections 2.8.4, "Atmospheric Dispersion," and 6.1, "Design Basis Accidents," of NUREG-0498, Supplement 2, Draft Final Environmental Statement Related to the Operation of Watts Bar Nuclear Plant, Unit 2 (ADAMS Accession No. ML112980199), October 2011, and in Section 11.3, "Gaseous Waste Management," of SSER 24, September 2011 (ADAMS Accession No. ML11277A148).

TVA stated, in the enclosure to its letter dated August 22, 2011 (ADAMS Accession No. ML112350646), that, during licensing of WBN Unit 1, it developed and used site-specific terrain adjustment factors (TAFs) to account for topography and diurnal-related factors in determining the dose to the maximum exposed individual. TVA applied these factors to the receptors within approximately 5 miles of the plant, as shown in FSAR Table 3.11-8. It did not apply TAFs to the $\chi/Q$ values used for determining the 50-mile total population dose for licensing Unit 1. It developed licensing submittals for Unit 2 on the same basis as for WBN Unit 1, and TAFs were not used in determining the 50-mile population dose. TVA provided a summary discussion and results of comparison evaluations in the enclosure as a further basis for determining that the 50-mile population doses presented in the FSAR are sufficiently conservative and that no additional correction factors (i.e., near-site TAFs) need be included. Based upon its assessment of the information provided by TVA and a site-specific review for WBN Unit 2, the NRC staff concludes that, for WBN Unit 2 only, it is acceptable, that TVA did not use TAFs to calculate the $\chi/Q$ and $D/Q$ values associated with the 16 radial sectors.

# 5 REACTOR COOLANT SYSTEM AND CONNECTED SYSTEMS

## 5.3 Reactor Vessel

*Disposition of Open Items (Appendix HH)*

### 5.3.1 Reactor Vessel Materials

#### Open Item 14

In Enclosure 1 of the Tennessee Valley Authority's (TVA's) letter dated July 31, 2010 (Agencywide Documents Access and Management System (ADAMS) Accession No. ML102290258), TVA responded to the U.S. Nuclear Regulatory Commission (NRC) staff's Request for Additional Information (RAI) 5.3.1-1, Question 1, and proposed changes to the pressure-temperature limits report (PTLR), including the addition of the reactor vessel (RV) surveillance capsule withdrawal schedule and a description of the RV surveillance program. In addition, TVA stated that the Watts Bar Nuclear Plant (WBN) Unit 2 PTLR is included in the WBN Unit 2 "System Description for the Reactor Coolant System" (WBN2-68-4001), which would be revised to reflect required revisions to the PTLR by September 17, 2010 (Supplemental Safety Evaluation Report (SSER) 22, Section 5.3.1, p 5-8). The staff identified **Open Item 14** to verify that TVA had revised the PTLR to include the RV surveillance capsule withdrawal schedule and RV surveillance program description.

In a letter dated April 6, 2011 (ADAMS Accession No. ML110980637), TVA stated that Revision 1 (effective August 12, 2010) of WBN2-68-4001 reflected the required revisions to the PTLR.

The staff concludes that TVA's response to Open Item 14 is acceptable because it confirms that TVA has revised the PTLR to include the RV surveillance program information. Therefore, **Open Item 14 is closed.**

#### Open Item 44

In response to RAI 5.3.1-1, Question 2, contained in Enclosure 1 to TVA's letter dated July 31, 2010 (ADAMS Accession No. ML102290258), TVA stated that the material test requirements and the acceptance standard use the nil-ductility reference temperature, $RT_{NDT}$, which is determined in accordance with American Society for Testing and Materials (ASTM) E208, "Standard Test Method for Conducting Drop-Weight Test to Determine Nil-Ductility Transition Temperature of Ferritic Steels." Since ASTM E208 is the standard for drop-weight testing, while NRC requirements for determination of $RT_{NDT}$ require a combination of drop-weight and Charpy V-notch ($C_v$) tests, the NRC staff required, in Open Item 44, that TVA provide additional information to clarify how it determined the initial and irradiated $RT_{NDT}$ (SSER 22, Section 5.3.1, pp 5-9, 5-11, 5-13, 5-17, 5-28, 5-29, 5-31, 5-32).

In a letter dated April 6, 2011 (ADAMS Accession No. ML110980637), in response to Open Item 44, TVA explained that the WBN Unit 2 RV fabricator used a combination of drop-weight and $C_v$ tests to determine the initial (unirradiated) $RT_{NDT}$ for the RV materials. The $C_v$ specimens were oriented in the tangential (strong) direction rather that the axial (weak) direction, as is required by the American Society of Mechanical Engineers (ASME) Boiler and Pressure Vessel Code (ASME Code), Section III, Subarticle NB-2300, which is referenced in Appendix G, "Fracture Toughness Requirements," to Title 10 of the *Code of Federal*

*Regulations* (10 CFR) Part 50, "Domestic Licensing of Production and Utilization Facilities," with respect to the method for determining the unirradiated $RT_{NDT}$. TVA explained that it designed the WBN Unit 2 RV in accordance with the ASME Code, Section II, 1971, addenda, which predate the current requirements for determining the unirradiated $RT_{NDT}$. However, it used the guidance in NRC Branch Technical Position (BTP) MTEB 5-2 to adjust the $C_v$ results to determine the equivalent properties in the weak direction, which it then used to determine the initial $RT_{NDT}$. In addition, it performed unirradiated $C_v$ tests on WBN Unit 2 RV surveillance program materials in both the weak and strong directions, and in conjunction with the drop-weight tests, to determine the unirradiated $RT_{NDT}$. These $C_v$ results showed that the initial $RT_{NDT}$ determination based on the $C_v$ tests in the strong direction, adjusted using BTP MTEB 5-2, are conservative.

TVA also stated that it determined the effects of irradiation on the WBN Unit 2 RV materials using $C_v$ specimens in the surveillance capsules, and that it only used drop-weight testing to determine the unirradiated $RT_{NDT}$.

The staff concludes that TVA's response to Open Item 44 is acceptable because it clarifies how it determined the initial (unirradiated) and irradiated $RT_{NDT}$, and because the methods TVA used are consistent with the guidance of BTP MTEB 5-2, which the staff finds acceptable for determining the fracture toughness properties of RVs fabricated before the current ASME Code, Section III, requirements for determining $RT_{NDT}$ came into effect. Therefore, **Open Item 44 is closed.**

### 5.3.2 Pressure-Temperature Limits

Open Item 45

TVA stated, in its response to RAI 5.3.2-2, dated July 31, 2010, that it would revise the PTLR to incorporate the cold overpressure mitigation system (COMS) arming temperature (SSER 22, Section 5.3.2, pp 5-28–29, 5-32). The staff identified Open Item 45 to verify incorporation of the COMS arming temperature into the PTLR.

In a letter dated April 6, 2011 (ADAMS Accession No. ML110980637), in response to Open Item 45, TVA stated that Revision 1 (effective August 12, 2010) to WBN2-68-4001 reflected the required revision to the PTLR. Appendix B, Section 3.2, "Arming Temperature," states, "COMS shall be armed when any RCS [reactor coolant system] cold leg temperature is ≤ 225 °F."

The staff concludes that TVA's response to Open Item 45 is acceptable because it confirms that TVA revised the PTLR to specify the COMS arming temperature. Therefore, **Open Item 45 is closed.**

Open Item 46

TVA did not include the low-temperature overpressure protection (LTOP) lift settings in the PTLR but provided them in its response to RAI 5.3.2-2 in its letter dated July 31, 2010. In its RAI response, TVA stated that it would revise the PTLR to incorporate the LTOP lift settings (SSER 22, Section 5.3.2, pp 5-28–29, 5-32). The staff identified Open Item 46 to verify incorporation of the LTOP settings into the PTLR.

In a letter dated April 6, 2011 (ADAMS Accession No. ML110980637), in response to Open Item 46, TVA stated that Revision 1 (effective August 12, 2010) to WBN2-68-4001 reflected the required revisions to the PTLR.  Appendix B, Table 3.1-1, "Watts Bar Unit 2 PORV [Power-Operated Relief Valve] Setpoints vs. Temperature," contains the LTOP lift settings.

The staff concludes that TVA's response to Open Item 46 is acceptable because it confirms that TVA revised the PTLR to include the LTOP lift settings into the PTLR.  Therefore, **Open Item 46 is closed.**

# 7 INSTRUMENTATION AND CONTROLS

## 7.5 Safety-Related Display Instrumentation

### 7.5.2 Postaccident Monitoring System

#### 7.5.2.2 Common Qualified Platform—Postaccident Monitoring System

*Disposition of Open Items (Appendix HH)*

### Open Item 72

Open Item 72 states, "The NRC staff should complete its review and evaluation of the additional information provided by TVA regarding the ICC [inadequate core cooling] instrumentation." The item was generated during the U.S. Nuclear Regulatory Commission (NRC) staff's review of the Tennessee Valley Authority's (TVA's) Watts Bar Nuclear (WBN) reactor in Section 4.4.8 of Supplemental Safety Evaluation Report (SSER) 23, issued July 2011.

The NRC staff documented its review of the Common Q postaccident monitoring system (PAMS) and ICC in Section 7.5.2.2 of SSER 23. The staff generated Open Items 94–111 (Appendix HH) during its review. Therefore, **Open Item 72 is closed,** because it is subsumed by Open Items 94–111.

### Open Item 95

Open Item 95 states, "TVA should update FSAR Table 7.1-1, 'Watts Bar Nuclear Plant NRC Regulatory Guide Conformance,' to reference IEEE Std. 603-1991 for the WBN Unit 2 Common Q PAMS."

In Table 7.1-1 of Final Safety Analysis Report (FSAR) Amendment 105, dated August 12, 2011, TVA stated the following:

> IEEE Std. 603-1991, "IEEE Standard Criteria for Safety Systems for Nuclear Power Generating Stations," (See Note 13).
>
> ...
> **Note 13 Common Q Post Accident Monitoring System (PAMS) Applicability**
> These Rules, Regulations and standards are applicable to the design of the Common Q PAMS system cabinets.

Based on the revised wording in FSAR Amendment 105, the NRC staff concludes that the open item has been adequately addressed. Therefore, **Open Item 95 is closed.**

### Open Item 96

Open Item 96 states, "TVA should (1) update FSAR Table 7.1-1 to include RG 1.100, Revision 3 for the Common Q PAMS, or (2) demonstrate that the Common Q PAMS is in conformance with RG 1.100, Revision 1, or (3) provide justification for not conforming."

By letter dated August 4, 2011 (Agencywide Documents Access and Management System (ADAMS) Accession No. ML11222A113), TVA responded to the open item, stating that it will add Regulatory Guide (RG) 1.100, "Seismic Qualification of Electric and Mechanical Equipment for Nuclear Power Plants," Revision 3, issued September 2009, to Table 7.1-1 for Common Q PAMS. In Table 7.1-1 of FSAR Amendment 105, TVA stated the following:

> Regulatory Guide 1.100, Revision 3, September 2009, "Seismic Qualification of Electric and Mechanical Equipment for Nuclear Power Plants" (See Notes 13, 14, and 16).
>
> ...
>
> **Note 13 Common Q Post Accident Monitoring System (PAMS) Applicability**
> These Rules, Regulations and standards are applicable to the design of the Common Q PAMS system cabinets.
>
> **Note 16 Conformance to Regulatory Guide 1.100, Revision 3 and IEEE 344-2004**
> The Common Q new design modules used in the PAMS; and the RM-1000 radiation monitors comply with IEEE 344-2004 and with Regulatory Guide 1.100 Revision 3 with the exception of issues associated with testing above 33Hz.

Based on the revised words in FSAR Amendment 105, the NRC staff concludes that the open item has been adequately addressed. Therefore, **Open Item 96 is closed.**

Open Item 97

Open Item 97 states, "TVA should demonstrate that the WBN Unit 2 Common Q PAMS is in conformance with RG 1.153, Revision 1 or provide justification for not conforming."

By letter dated August 4, 2011 (ADAMS Accession No. ML11222A113), TVA responded to this open item, stating that it will add RG 1.153, "Criteria for Safety Systems," Revision 1, issued June 1996, to FSAR Table 7.1-1 for Common Q PAMS. In Table 7.1-1 of FSAR Amendment 105, TVA stated the following:

> Regulatory Guide 1.153, Revision 1, June 1996, "Criteria for Safety Systems" (See Note 13).
>
> ...
>
> **Note 13 Common Q Post Accident Monitoring System (PAMS) Applicability**
> These Rules, Regulations and standards are applicable to the design of the Common Q PAMS system cabinets.

Based on the revised words in FSAR Amendment 105, the NRC staff concludes that the open item has been adequately addressed. Therefore, **Open Item 97 is closed.**

Open Item 99

Open Item 99 states, "TVA should update FSAR Table 7.1-1 to reference IEEE 7-4.3.2-2003 as being applicable to the WBN Unit 2 Common Q PAMS."

By letter dated August 4, 2011 (ADAMS Accession No. ML11222A113), TVA responded to this action item, stating that it would add Institute of Electrical and Electronics Engineers (IEEE) Standard (Std.) 7-4.3.2, "Application Criteria for Programmable Digital Computer Systems in Safety Systems of Nuclear Power Generating Stations," to Table 7.1-1 for Common Q PAMS. Table 7.1-1 of FSAR Amendment 105 states the following:

IEEE Std. 7-4.3.2-2003 "Application Criteria for Programmable Digital Computer Systems in Safety Systems of Nuclear Power Generating Stations" (See Notes 13 and 18).

...

**Note 13 Common Q Post Accident Monitoring System (PAMS) Applicability**
These Rules, Regulations and standards are applicable to the design of the Common Q PAMS system cabinets.

...

**Note 18 Conformance to IEEE 7-4.3.2-2003**
The Common Q PAMS meets the applicable requirements of IEEE 7-4.3.2-2003, except as noted below:

    1. The quality program is in accordance with WCAP-16096-NP-1A "Software Program Manual" (SPM).

    2. The commercial item dedication program is in accordance with the Westinghouse 10CFR50.54 Appendix B program."

However, in its audit report dated April 27, 2011 (ADAMS Accession No. ML110980761), the NRC staff identified several examples of practices that do not comply with the software program manual, or where Westinghouse no longer followed the software program manual. The software program manual also contains criteria for commercial-grade dedication. Based on the revised wording in FSAR Amendment 105, the NRC staff concluded that TVA did not adequately address the item.

By letter dated September 30, 2011 (ADAMS Accession No. ML11286A037, Enclosure 1, Item 17), TVA stated the following:

The inclusion of Note 18 was caused by a misinterpretation of the requirements of RG 1.152 Revision 3 as it applied to IEEE 7-4.3.2 2003 by the TVA reviewer. Discussion with the NRC reviewer determined that the note was not required. Note 18 was removed in FSAR Amendment 106.

Since TVA updated the FSAR to include reference IEEE Std. 7-4.3.2-2003 as applicable to the WBN Unit 2 Common Q PAMS, **Open Item 99 is closed.**

Open Item 100

Open Item 100 states, "TVA should update FSAR Table 7.1-1 to reference RG 1.168, Revision 1, IEEE Std. 1012-1998, and IEEE 1028-1997 as being applicable to the WBN Unit 2 Common Q PAMS."

By letter dated August 4, 2011 (ADAMS Accession No. ML11222A113), TVA responded to this open item, stating that it would add RG 1.168, "Verification, Validation, Reviews, and Audits for Digital Computer Software Used in Safety Systems of Nuclear Power Plants," Revision 1, issued February 2004; IEEE Std. 1012-1998, "IEEE Standard for Software Verification and Validation"; and IEEE Std. 1028-1997, "IEEE Standard for Software Reviews," to Table 7.1-1 for Common Q PAMS. In Table 7.1-1 of FSAR Amendment 105, TVA stated the following:

Regulatory Guide 1.168, Revision 1, February 2004, "Verification, Validation, Reviews, and Audits for Digital Computer Software Used in Safety Systems of

Nuclear Power Plants" (See Note 13)...IEEE Std. 1012-1998, "IEEE Standard for Software Verification and Validation" (See Note 13). IEEE Std. 1028-1997, "IEEE Standard for Software Reviews" (See Note 13).

...

**Note 13 Common Q Post Accident Monitoring System (PAMS) Applicability**
These Rules, Regulations and standards are applicable to the design of the Common Q PAMS system cabinets.

Based on the revised words in FSAR Amendment 105, the NRC staff concludes that the open item has been adequately addressed. Therefore, **Open Item 100 is closed.**

Open Item 102

Open Item 102 states, "TVA should update FSAR Table 7.1-1 to reference RG 1.209 and IEEE Std. 323-2003 as being applicable to the WBN Unit 2 Common Q PAMS."

By letter dated August 4, 2011 (ADAMS Accession No. ML11222A113), TVA responded to this open item, stating that it would add RG 1.209, "Guidelines for Environmental Qualification of Safety-Related Computer-Based Instrumentation and Control Systems in Nuclear Power Plants," issued March 2007, and IEEE Std. 323-2003, "IEEE Standard for Qualifying Class 1E Equipment for Nuclear Power Generating Stations," to Table 7.1-1. In Table 7.1-1 of FSAR Amendment 105, TVA stated the following:

Regulatory Guide 1.209, Revision 0, March 2007, "Guidelines for Environmental Qualification of Safety-Related Computer-Based Instrumentation and Control Systems in Nuclear Power Plants" (See Note 13)...IEEE Std. 323-2003, "IEEE Standard for Qualifying Class 1E Equipment for Nuclear Power Generating Stations," (See Note 13).

...

**Note 13 Common Q Post Accident Monitoring System (PAMS) Applicability**
These Rules, Regulations and standards are applicable to the design of the Common Q PAMS system cabinets.

Based on the revised words in FSAR Amendment 105, the NRC staff concludes that the open item has been adequately addressed. Therefore, **Open Item 102 is closed.**

Open Item 103

Open Item 103 states, "TVA should demonstrate that the WBN Unit 2 Common Q PAMS conforms to RG 1.209 and IEEE Std. 323-2003 or provide justification for not conforming."

By letter dated August 4, 2011 (ADAMS Accession No. ML11222A113), TVA responded to this open item; Attachment 3 to the letter included the requested evaluation.

Based on its review of the information submitted by TVA, the staff concluded that TVA provided an adequate evaluation of conformance with RG 1.209 and IEEE Std. 323-2003. Therefore, **Open Item 103 is closed.**

Open Item 104

Open Item 104 states, "The NRC staff will review the WEC [Westinghouse Electric Corporation] self-assessment to verify that the WBN Unit 2 PAMS complies with the V&V [verification and validation] requirements in the SPM or that deviations from the requirements are adequately justified."

By letter dated June 10, 2011 (ADAMS Accession No. ML11167A110), TVA provided information to address this item (see letter item 15, "NRC Common Q PAMS Audit Action Items Response"). The information provided and the information subsequently reviewed demonstrate that Westinghouse did not consistently follow the software program manual and that Westinghouse did not plan and document these deviations beforehand; however, TVA did provide sufficient information to allow the NRC staff to determine, with reasonable assurance, that the Common Q PAMS does not pose a threat to public health and safety. Therefore, **Open Item 104 is closed.**

Open Item 106

Open Item 106 states, "TVA should provide to the NRC staff documentation to confirm that the final WBN Unit 2 Common Q PAMS SRS [system requirements specification] is independently reviewed."

By letter dated June 10, 2011 (ADAMS Accession No. ML11167A110), TVA responded to "NRC Request (Item Number 372)," documenting why it concluded that the reviews were independent. The information provided was essentially an affirmation that the documents were independently reviewed. The Westinghouse internal guidance (reviewed during the NRC audit documented at ADAMS Accession No. ML110980761) is inconsistent on how to document that a review was an "independent review—satisfying Appendix B" versus a more informal review. However, the NRC staff considers that the affirmation provided by TVA in its letter dated June 10, 2011, is sufficient; therefore, **Open Item 106 is closed.**

Open Item 107

Open Item 107 states, "TVA should provide to the NRC staff documentation to confirm that the final WBN Unit 2 Common Q PAMS SDDs [software design documents] are independently reviewed."

By letter dated June 10, 2011 (ADAMS Accession No. ML11167A110), TVA responded to "NRC Request (Item Number 373)," documenting why it concluded that the reviews were independent. The information provided was essentially an affirmation that the documents were independently reviewed. The Westinghouse internal guidance (reviewed during the NRC audit documented at ADAMS Accession No. ML110980761) is inconsistent on how to document that a review was an "independent review—satisfying Appendix B" versus a more informal review. However, the NRC staff considers the affirmation provided by TVA in its letter dated June 10, 2011, to be sufficient; therefore, **Open Item 107 is closed.**

Open Item 109

Open Item 109 states, "TVA should demonstrate to the NRC staff acceptable data storm testing of the Common Q PAMS."

By letter dated June 10, 2011 (ADAMS Accession No. ML11167A110), TVA responded to "18. NRC Verbal Request," which stated the following:

> Watts Bar Unit 2 Post Accident Monitoring System went through a Data Storm Test to verify that the safety related functions of the system driven by the Advant

Controller 160 (AC 160) and the safety related indications monitored on the Operator Module (OM) located in the Main Control Room (MCR) are not affected when the Ethernet network interface of the Maintenance and Test Panel (MTP) is under data storm conditions. This test was requested by TVA.

The purpose of the data storm test was to test the ability of the MTP to handle the possible volume of traffic generated by a broadcast storm without impacting the safety functions. A broadcast storm occurs when a large number of broadcast packets are received. Forwarding these packets can cause the network to slow down or to time out.

Another objective of the data storm test was to test the ability of the MTP to handle malformed packets possibly generated by a data storm without impacting the safety functions.

TVA also described the pass/fail criteria and associated results. The PAMS continued to perform its safety function during the data storm testing, as demonstrated by its meeting the acceptance criteria.

Based on its review of the information provided by TVA, the NRC staff concludes that the open item was acceptably addressed. Therefore, **Open Item 109 is closed.**

7.5.2.2.3.9.2.5 IEEE Std. 603-1991, Clause 5.6, Independence

In Section 7.5.2.2.3.9.2.5 of SSER 23, issued July 2011, the NRC staff concluded that the Common Q PAMS meets the acceptance criteria for independence and the requirements of Clause 5.6; therefore, the PAMS is acceptable.

Core exit thermocouples (CETs) are bundled together with the non-Class 1E self-powered neutron detectors in the mineral insulated cable and thus do not meet the separation requirements between safety- and nonsafety-related equipment in IEEE Std. 384-1981, "IEEE Standard Criteria for Independence of Class 1E Equipment and Circuits." The NRC staff documented its separation/isolation evaluation for the CETs in Section 7.7.1.9 of SSER 24, issued September 2011.

7.5.2.3 High-Range Containment Area Radiation Monitors

*Disposition of Open Items (Appendix HH)*

Open Item 78

Open Item 78 states, "TVA intends to issue a revised calculation reflecting that the TID [total integrated dose] in the control room is less than $1\times10^3$ rads, which will be evaluated by the NRC staff."

TVA's letter dated August 4, 2011 (ADAMS Accession No. ML11222A113), responded to the open item, and Enclosure 1 to the letter provided TVA's supporting calculation (Calculation No. WBNAPS3-127, Revision 0). TVA stated that the TID for the main control room, where the radiation monitors are located, is 362.76 rads. This radiation dose is acceptable to the NRC staff for mild environments according to the guidance in RG 1.209. Based on its review of the information provided in TVA's letter dated August 4, 2011, and the calculation summary, the staff concluded that TVA provided an adequate response. Therefore, **Open Item 78 is closed.**

## 7.7 Control Systems Not Required for Safety

### 7.7.1 System Description

#### 7.7.1.9 In-Core Instrumentation System

*Disposition of Open Items (Appendix HH)*

Open Item 119

Open Item 119 states, "TVA should submit WNA-CN-00157-WBT, Revision 0, to the NRC by letter. The NRC staff should confirm by review of WNA-CN-00157-WBT, Revision 0, that no credible source of faulting can negatively impact the CETs or PAMS train."

In Enclosure 1 and in Attachment 2 to its letter dated September 1, 2011 (ADAMS Accession No. ML11257A048), TVA responded to this open item. Attachment 2 included a copy of Westinghouse analysis WNA-CN-00157-WBT, Revision 0, "Watts Bar 2 Incore Instrument System (IIS) Signal Processing System (SPS) Isolation Requirements." The analysis shows the following:

1. No fault originating either within the WINCISE (Westinghouse INCore Information, Surveillance, and Engineering system) signal processing system (SPS) cabinet or electrical surges on the input power lines or output communications link can result in fault voltage affecting CET signals.

2. Inadvertent disconnection or failures of any IITA (in-core instrumentation thimble assembly) emitter wire or wires at the WINCISE SPS cabinet, or anywhere in the cabling between the IITA seal table connector and the WINCISE SPS cabinet, will not cause voltage charge-up on the emitter wire to exceed 600 volts direct current during worst case (full-power) plant operation, thus preventing the fault voltage from affecting the associated CET.

3. For large input overvoltage conditions on the 120-volt alternating current (Vac) input instrument bus used in both the SPS cabinet and associated PAMS train, the SPS will not cause any failure within the PAMS train that would not otherwise occur as a direct result of the overvoltage condition within the PAMS power supply.

The impact of a failed CET on a PAMS channel is addressed in Westinghouse analysis WNA-AR-00180-WBT-P, Revision 2, "Failure Modes and Effects Analysis (FMEA) for the Post Accident Monitoring System," page 3-6, in TVA's letter dated March 2, 2011 (ADAMS Accession No. ML110620411).

Based on the analysis results, the NRC staff concludes that TVA adequately addressed the issue, and **Open Item 119 is closed.**

Open Item 120

Open Item 120 states, "TVA should confirm to the NRC staff that the maximum over-voltage or surge voltage that could affect the system is 264 VAC, assuming that the power supply cable to the SPS cabinet is not routed with other cables greater than 264 VAC."

In Enclosure 1 and in Attachments 2 and 5 to its letter dated September 1, 2011 (ADAMS Accession No. ML11257A048), TVA responded to this open item. The information provided by TVA confirms that 264 Vac is the estimated maximum voltage, or surge-voltage, that could affect WINCISE. Furthermore, the equipment qualification for the WINCISE SPS, provided in Attachment 5, shows that the SPS cabinets can withstand a maximum surge of 4,000 volts with no loss of function after the surge.

However, TVA's response did not confirm that the power supply cable to the WINCISE SPS cabinet would not be routed with other cables carrying greater than 264 Vac. TVA must confirm that the power supply cable to the SPS cabinet is not routed with other cables with voltage greater than 264 Vac. **Open Item 120 remains open.**

Open Item 122

Open Item 122 states, "TVA should confirm to the NRC staff that different divisions of safety power are supplied to the IIS SPS cabinets, with the power cables routed in separate shielded conduits."

In Enclosure 1 to its letter dated September 1, 2011 (ADAMS Accession No. ML11257A048), TVA confirmed that different divisions of safety power are supplied to the IIS SPS cabinets, with the power cables routed in separate shielded conduits. Therefore, the NRC staff concludes that TVA adequately addressed the issue, and **Open Item 122 is closed.**

Open Item 124

Open Item 124 states, "While the BEACON datalink on the Application server can connect to either BEACON machine, only BEACON A is used for communication. TVA should clarify to the NRC staff whether automatic switchover to the other server is not permitted."

In Enclosure 1 to its letter dated September 1, 2011 (ADAMS Accession No. ML11257A048), TVA explained that the feature to automatically switch over to BEACON B is not configured for WBN Unit 2, and the BEACON datalink on the application server can only connect to BEACON A. TVA provided further information in Attachment 3 to its letter dated June 10, 2011 (ADAMS Accession No. ML11167A110). The NRC staff reviewed the information provided in TVA's letters dated June 10 and September 1, 2011, and concluded that its response was acceptable. Therefore, **Open Item 124 is closed.**

Open Item 128

Open Item 128 states, "TVA should submit the seismic qualification test report procedures and results for the SPS cabinets to the NRC staff for review."

In Enclosure 1 and in Attachment 5 to its letter dated September 1, 2011 (ADAMS Accession No. ML11257A048), TVA responded to this open item. Attachment 5 includes a copy of the Westinghouse report EQ-QR-39-WBT, Revision 0, "Equipment Qualification Summary Report for WINCISE Signal Processing System." This summary report describes the seismic qualification test performed and the results obtained. The WINCISE SPS cabinet maintained structural integrity without any component detachment throughout the test program and thus complied with WBN Unit 2 seismic qualification specification WB-DC-40-31.2, with testing performed in accordance with NRC RG 1.100, IEEE Std. 344-1975, and IEEE Std. 344-1987, "IEEE Recommended Practice for Seismic Qualification of Class 1E Equipment for Nuclear Power Generating Stations." Based on the information in the summary report, the NRC staff concludes that TVA adequately addressed the issue, and **Open Item 128 is closed.**

Open Item 130

Open Item 130 states, "TVA should provide a summary to the NRC staff of the EMC [electromagnetic compatibility] qualification test results of the SPS cabinets."

In Enclosure 1 and in Attachment 5 to its letter dated September 1, 2011 (ADAMS Accession No. ML11257A048), TVA responded to this open item. Attachment 5 includes a copy of the Westinghouse report EQ-QR-39-WBT, Revision 0, "Equipment Qualification Summary Report for WINCISE Signal Processing System." This summary report describes the EMC qualification test performed and the results obtained. The report states that the WINCISE SPS cabinet successfully complied with the emissions requirements of NRC RG 1.180, Revision 1, "Guidelines for Evaluating Electromagnetic and Radio-Frequency Interference in Safety-Related Instrumentation and Control Systems," and the supplemental-surge-withstand testing required in WNA-CN-00157-WBT. Therefore, the NRC staff concludes that TVA adequately addressed the issue, and **Open Item 130 is closed.**

# 11 RADIOACTIVE WASTE SYSTEM

## 11.3 Gaseous Waste Management

In Section 11.3 of Supplemental Safety Evaluation Report (SSER) Supplement 24 (Agencywide Documents Access and Management System (ADAMS) Accession No. ML11277A148), issued September 2011, to the safety evaluation report (SER) (NUREG-0847, "Safety Evaluation Report Related to the Operation of Watts Bar Nuclear Plant, Units 1 and 2," issued June 1982), the staff of the U.S. Nuclear Regulatory Commission (NRC) documented its evaluation of Tennessee Valley Authority's (TVA's) calculated doses to members of the public as revised by Final Safety Analysis Report (FSAR) Amendments 95 through 104. The staff concluded that the Watts Bar Nuclear Plant (WBN) Unit 2 design meets the dose limits in Title 10 of the *Code of Federal Regulations* (10 CFR) Part 20, "Standards for Protection Against Radiation," and the design objectives in 10 CFR Part 50, "Domestic Licensing of Production and Utilization Facilities," Appendix I, "Numerical Guides for Design Objectives and Limiting Conditions for Operation to Meet the Criterion 'As Low as is Reasonably Achievable' for Radioactive Material in Light-Water-Cooled Nuclear Power Reactor Effluents," Sections II.A, II.B, and II.C. However, the revised doses did not support a conclusion that the criteria for gaseous effluents in RM 50-2 (as annexed to Appendix I to 10 CFR Part 50) are met. This was documented as **Open Item 135** (Appendix HH). In response, by letter dated July 28, 2011, TVA provided a cost-benefit analysis, as required by 10 CFR Part 50, Appendix I, Section II.D, to demonstrate that a sufficient reduction in the annual collective dose to the public within a 50-mile radius would not be achieved by reasonable enhancements to the design of the WBN gaseous effluent processing systems.

TVA performed the cost-benefit analysis for several potential enhancements to the gaseous radwaste systems in accordance with the methodology presented in Regulatory Guide (RG) 1.110, "Cost-Benefit Analysis for Radwaste Systems for Light-Water-Cooled Nuclear Power Reactors (for Comment)," issued March 1976. In lieu of expressing the cost and benefits in terms of dollars, TVA's analysis compares the potential annual collective dose (person-rem) saving by the specific system enhancement to a threshold dose indicated by the annualized cost of the enhancement (e.g., at $1,000/person-rem, an annualized cost of $2,000 would indicate that an annual collective dose savings of at least 2 person-rem would be required for the enhancement to have a favorable cost-benefit ratio of less than 1.0). The analysis considered the total body and thyroid collective doses caused by the design-basis gaseous effluent releases to the population anticipated to live within 50 miles of the plant in the year 2040.

TVA calculated an annual collective total body dose of 6.68 person-rem resulting from gaseous effluent releases with the current radwaste system design. Using the methods in RG 1.110, TVA calculated the lowest threshold value for a gaseous enhancement at 6.32 person-rem. Since this threshold dose is below the total gaseous effluent dose, the licensee was required to consider specific dose savings associated with each system enhancement. The lowest cost enhancement included in RG 1.110 is the addition of a steam generator blowdown flash tank vent routed to the main condenser. The addition of this vent would only lower turbine building vent releases. TVA calculated the total body dose from all turbine building vent releases to be 0.033 person-rem. This is much less than the threshold value, so the enhancement is not cost beneficial. The next lowest cost enhancement is the addition of a 600-cubic foot ($ft^3$) gas decay tank. TVA calculated the threshold value of this enhancement to be 7.46 person-rem. This is higher than the 6.68 person-rem total body dose from all WBN gaseous effluent releases.

Therefore, adding this enhancement was not determined to be cost beneficial. Consistent with the RG 1.110 methodology, no additional total body dose reductions needed to be considered.

TVA calculated an annual collective thyroid dose of 13.0 person-rem from gaseous effluent releases with the current radwaste system design. Consistent with the RG 1.110 methodology, TVA evaluated the following seven enhancements relative to the thyroid dose in order of cost from lowest to highest:

1. Routing the steam generator blowdown flash tank vent to the main condenser: The collective thyroid dose from the turbine building vent of 0.354 person-rem is significantly below the 6.32 person-rem threshold value for adding the flash tank vent. Therefore, this enhancement is not cost beneficial.

2. The addition of a 600-ft$^3$ waste gas decay tank: This enhancement has already been incorporated in the plant design. WBN already has nine 600-ft$^3$ gas decay tanks with sufficient capacity to store gaseous waste to a minimum of 60 days before release. The decayed gases are discharged through a charcoal adsorber/high-efficiency particulate air (HEPA) filter and a radiation monitor before being released through the shield building stack. Adding a tenth gas decay tank will not reduce the thyroid dose. The threshold value of 7.46 person-rem was found to be in excess of the potential dose reduction.

3. The addition of a 1,000-cubic-foot-per-minute (cfm) charcoal/HEPA filter to the auxiliary building ventilation system: TVA calculated a threshold value for this enhancement at 7.58 person-rem for a single 1,000-cfm filter unit. This is lower than the 9.15 thyroid person-rem resulting from auxiliary building vent releases. However, the auxiliary building vent air flow rate is 84,000 cfm. Treating only 1,000 cfm of the total release would impact less than 2 percent of the resulting dose. Thus, in reality, the threshold value for the auxiliary building would be many times the 7.58 value, since more than 50 1,000-cfm filter packages would be needed to effectively filter the auxiliary building gaseous effluent. Therefore, this enhancement would not be cost beneficial.

4. A charcoal/HEPA filter to the main condenser vacuum exhaust: The threshold value for this modification was 7.69 person-rem. This exceeds the thyroid dose release from the turbine building. This enhancement would not be cost beneficial.

5. A 3-ton charcoal adsorber to the shield building vent: RG 1.110 assumes that this enhancement would be located in the turbine building and appended to the waste gas decay system. The threshold dose value for this enhancement is 8.77 person-rem. However, TVA stated that the WBN waste gas decay system is located in the auxiliary building and is vented through the shield building stack. The total annual cost of placing the filter in the auxiliary building would be higher than the turbine building placement assumed in RG 1.110. Notwithstanding that issue, TVA calculated the thyroid population dose from the reactor building (which is the location of the shield building vent) to be 3.48 person-rem. The threshold value is greater than the potential dose reduction. Therefore this enhancement is not cost beneficial.

6. An air ejector charcoal/HEPA filtration unit: WBN Unit 2 does not have air ejectors but uses condenser vacuum pumps. TVA already evaluated the addition of filters on the vacuum pump discharge and showed that it was not cost beneficial. This enhancement has a higher cost and was eliminated from further consideration.

7. A 15,000-cfm HEPA filtration system for the turbine building or the auxiliary building: The threshold value for a single filter unit was 16.9 person-rem. The threshold value for this enhancement exceeds the 13.0 person-rem total thyroid population dose. Therefore, consistent with the RG 1.110 methodology, TVA did not consider further enhancements to the gaseous effluent processing systems.

*Conclusions*

The NRC staff performed an independent cost-benefit analysis to verify that these gaseous effluent treatment enhancements are not cost effective. The annualized costs of the gaseous effluent system enhancements identified by TVA were determined in accordance with the guidance in RG 1.110. Using the GASPAR input parameters described in SSER 24, the staff calculated the 50-mile radius collective doses (expected for the year 2040) listed in Table 11.1.

**Table 11.1 NRC Staff's 50-Mile Collective
Population Dose per Release Source
(Person-Rem)**

| ORGAN | AUXILIARY | TURBINE | CONTAINMENT | TOTAL |
|---|---|---|---|---|
| Total Body | 2.92E+00 | 4.19E-02 | 3.15E+00 | 6.11E+00 |
| Thyroid | 1.04E+01 | 4.16E-01 | 3.47E+00 | 1.42E+01 |

In addition, the staff assumed the minimum capital recovery factor listed in Table A-6 of RG 1.110, which resulted in lower annualized costs of the proposed effluent treatment enhancements by about 10 percent. Despite slightly higher collective doses and somewhat lower annualized costs, the staff's analysis verified the TVA conclusions above, that no enhancements evaluated result in a favorable cost-benefit ratio. Therefore, the licensee is not required to include these enhancements in the WBN gaseous effluent systems.

Based on the NRC staff's evaluation, as documented in SSER 24, and the results of the cost-benefit analysis, the staff concludes that the WBN effluent systems can maintain gaseous releases within the design objectives in 10 CFR Part 50, Appendix I, Sections II.A, II.B, and II.C, and are as low as is reasonably achievable, as required in 10 CFR Part 50, Appendix I, Section II.D. Therefore, **Open Item 135 is closed.** The results of the cost-benefit analysis required by 10 CFR Part 50, Appendix I, subsection II.D, should be provided in the WBN Unit 2 FSAR. Upon receipt of the updated FSAR, the NRC staff will confirm that the update has been made by TVA. This is **Open Item 139** (Appendix HH).

# 13 CONDUCT OF OPERATIONS

## 13.1 Organizational Structure of Applicant

### 13.1.3 Plant Staff Organization

*Disposition of Open Items (Appendix HH)*

Open Item 11 (Appendix HH) states the following:

> The plant administrative procedures should clearly state that, when the Assistant Shift Engineer assumes his duties as Fire Brigade Leader, his control room duties are temporarily assumed by the Shift Supervisor (Shift Engineer), or by another SRO [senior reactor operator], if one is available. The plant administrative procedures should clearly describe this transfer of control room duties.

In Enclosure 1 of its letter dated August 15, 2011 (Agencywide Documents Access and Management System Accession No. ML11230A385), the Tennessee Valley Authority provided its revised Watts Bar Nuclear Plant Unit 1/Unit 2 as-designed fire protection report. The U.S. Nuclear Regulatory Commission staff reviewed Section 9.1, "Fire Brigade Staffing," of the fire protection report and concluded that, because it ensures that the fire brigade will not use members of the minimum shift crew, there is no need for an administrative procedure to describe a transfer of control room duties. Therefore, **Open Item 11 is closed.**

# 15    ACCIDENT ANALYSIS

## 15.4    Radiological Consequences of Accidents

To evaluate the effectiveness of the engineered safety features proposed for Watts Bar Nuclear Plant (WBN) Unit 2 and to ensure that the radiological consequences of these accidents meet the applicable dose criteria, the staff of the U.S. Nuclear Regulatory Commission (NRC) reviewed the Tennessee Valley Authority's (TVA's) analyses for the loss of alternating current (ac) power to the plant auxiliary equipment, the waste gas decay tank rupture, the loss-of-coolant accident (LOCA), the main steamline break (MSLB), the steam generator tube rupture (SGTR), and the fuel-handling accident (FHA). TVA did not provide an updated detailed evaluation for the rod ejection accident because this accident is bounded by the LOCA. TVA calculated accident doses for the exclusion area boundary (EAB), the outer boundary of the low-population zone (LPZ), and the control room (CR). Table 15.1 of this supplemental safety evaluation report (SSER) shows TVA's calculated doses for the analyzed accidents.

The atmospheric dispersion factors ($\chi$/Q) used in the WBN analyses are those that the NRC staff discussed in Section 2.3.4 of the safety evaluation report (SER) (NUREG-0847, "Safety Evaluation Report Related to the Operation of Watts Bar Nuclear Plant, Units 1 and 2," issued June 1982) and in its SSERs. The meteorological models described in the NRC regulatory guides (RGs) referenced in these analyses are appropriately modified by those presented in RG 1.145, "Atmospheric Dispersion Models for Potential Accident Consequence Assessments at Nuclear Power Plants," Revision 1, issued February 1983.

The NRC staff reviewed WBN Unit 2 Final Safety Analysis Report (FSAR) Section 15.5, "Environmental Consequences of Accidents," using the criteria in NUREG-75/087, "Standard Review Plan for the Review of Safety Analysis Reports for Nuclear Power Plants: LWR Edition," Revision 2, issued May 1980. Since the acceptance criteria in NUREG-0800, "Standard Review Plan for the Review of Safety Analysis Reports for Nuclear Power Plants" (SRP), are not significantly different from those in NUREG-75/087, the NRC staff's conclusions in this SSER section are also in accordance with the acceptance criteria of the SRP.

The NRC staff previously reviewed the radiological dose consequence analyses performed by TVA for WBN Units 1 and 2 and documented the results of the review in the SER and in SSERs through SSER 18, issued October 1995. Subsequently, the NRC issued WBN Unit 1 an operating license, and it began commercial operation in 1996. Since the initial NRC staff review, the licensee made changes to the radiological dose consequence analyses for Unit 1 using Title 10 of the *Code of Federal Regulations* (10 CFR) 50.59, "Changes, Tests, and Experiments," and the license amendment process in 10 CFR 50.90, "Application for Amendment of License, Construction Permit, or Early Site Permit." For this SSER, the NRC staff used the current licensing basis (CLB) for Unit 1 as a benchmark for acceptability of the Unit 2 analyses and addressed those revised Unit 1 parameters and assumptions that are different for Unit 2.

TVA addresses the dose consequences of the following seven postulated design-basis accidents in Section 15.5, "Environmental Consequences of Accidents," of the WBN Unit 2 FSAR:

(1)    loss of alternating current (ac) power to the plant auxiliaries
(2)    waste gas decay tank rupture
(3)    LOCA

(4)     MSLB
(5)     SGTR
(6)     FHA
(7)     rod ejection accident

15.4.1 Loss-of-Coolant Accident

The NRC staff previously reviewed the LOCA radiological dose consequence analysis performed for WBN Units 1 and 2 and documented the results of this review in the SER and in SSERs 5, 9, 15, and 18 (issued October 1995). Subsequently, the NRC issued WBN Unit 1 an operating license, and it began commercial operation in 1996. Since the initial NRC staff review, TVA made changes to the LOCA radiological dose consequence analysis for Unit 1 using the 10 CFR 50.59 change process and the 10 CFR 50.90 license amendment process. For this SSER, the NRC staff used the CLB LOCA assumptions for Unit 1 as a benchmark for acceptability of the Unit 2 LOCA analysis and addressed the following revised Unit 1 parameters and assumptions that are different for Unit 2.

*Time-Dependent Emergency Gas Treatment System Flow Rates*

The time-dependent emergency gas treatment system (EGTS) flow rates for Units 1 and 2 are revised as a result of an alternative single failure scenario resulting in one pressure control train in full exhaust to the shield building exhaust stack while the other train remains functional. Both EGTS fans are in service until operator action is taken to place one fan in standby between 1 and 2 hours after the accident.

The Unit 1 and Unit 2 EGTS flow rates are based on separate analyses of ventilation system calculations reflecting the physical differences between the units.

*Source Term*

The source term used in the LOCA dose consequence analysis performed for Unit 2 differs from the Unit 1 LOCA source term, because the Unit 1 source term is based on a tritium core, whereas the Unit 2 source term is based on a standard core. The Unit 2 LOCA dose consequence analysis did not consider tritium-producing burnable absorber rods (TPBARs), since TVA did not request permission to produce tritium in Unit 2.

The NRC staff review concluded that the aforementioned unit-specific changes used to evaluate the WBN Unit 2 LOCA analysis are based on physical differences in the units, unit-specific operational differences, or updated information that has been accepted by the NRC staff for use in dose consequence analyses. The TVA evaluation concluded that the radiological consequences resulting from a postulated LOCA at the EAB, LPZ, and CR comply with the reference values and the CR dose criterion provided in 10 CFR 100.11, "Determination of Exclusion Area, Low-Population Zone, and Population Center Distance," and in 10 CFR Part 50, "Domestic Licensing of Production and Utilization Facilities," Appendix A, "General Design Criteria for Nuclear Power Plants," General Design Criterion (GDC) 19, "Control Room," as well as with the accident-specific dose guidelines specified in the SRP. The NRC staff's review concluded that TVA used analyses, assumptions, and inputs consistent with those described in the SRP. The NRC staff concluded that the assumptions presented in Table 15.2 and TVA's calculated dose results in Table 15.1 of this SSER were acceptable. The NRC staff concludes that TVA's estimates of the dose consequences of a design-basis LOCA are in accordance with the SRP acceptance criteria.

## 15.4.2 Main Steamline Break Outside Containment

The NRC staff previously reviewed the MSLB radiological dose consequence analysis performed for WBN Units 1 and 2 and documented the results of this review in the SER and in SSER 15 (issued June 1995). Subsequently, the NRC issued WBN Unit 1 an operating license, and it began commercial operation in 1996. Since the initial NRC staff review, the licensee made changes to the MSLB radiological dose consequence analysis for Unit 1 using the 10 CFR 50.59 change process and the 10 CFR 50.90 license amendment process. For this SSER, the NRC staff used the CLB MSLB assumptions for Unit 1 as a benchmark for acceptability of the Unit 2 MSLB analysis and addressed the following revised Unit 1 parameters and assumptions that are different for Unit 2.

### Steam Release Values

Unit 2 steam release values are different from Unit 1 values because the Unit 1 steam generators have been replaced by differently designed models. The volume of steam release in Unit 2 reflects the use of the original steam generators (OSGs).

### Iodine Spike Assumptions

For Unit 2, the short-term maximum allowable dose equivalent iodine-131 (DEI) value is 14 microcuries/gram ($\mu$Ci/gm). TVA has informed the NRC staff (reference Agencywide Documents Access and Management System (ADAMS) Accession No. ML11252A530) that it will submit a license amendment request to revise the Unit 1 technical specification (TS) short-term maximum allowable DEI from 21 $\mu$Ci/gm to 14 $\mu$Ci/gm. This change is necessary, since the dose conversion factors (DCFs) were changed from International Commission on Radiological Protection (ICRP)-2, "Permissible Dose for Internal Radiation," 1959, values to the values in RG 1.109, "Calculation of Annual Doses to Man from Routine Releases of Reactor Effluents for the Purpose of Evaluating Compliance with 10 CFR Part 50, Appendix I," Revision 1, issued October 1977. The Unit 1 TS require that RG 1.109 be used to determine the DEI. With this change, the short-term maximum allowable DEI value of 14 $\mu$Ci/gm will be consistent for both WBN Unit 1 and Unit 2. The NRC staff has endorsed the use of the DCFs from RG 1.109 in dose consequence analyses.

### Atmospheric Dispersion Factors

The Unit 2 atmospheric dispersion coefficients are based on a release from the Unit 2 vent valve stacks to the emergency CR intake.

The NRC staff review found that the aforementioned unit-specific changes used to evaluate the WBN Unit 2 MSLB analysis are based on physical differences in the units, unit-specific operational differences, or updated information that has been accepted by the NRC staff for use in dose consequence analyses. The TVA evaluation concluded that the radiological consequences resulting from the postulated MSLB at the EAB, LPZ, and CR comply with the reference values and the CR dose criterion provided in 10 CFR 100.11 and 10 CFR Part 50, Appendix A, GDC 19, as well as with the accident-specific dose guidelines specified in the SRP. The NRC staff concluded that TVA used analyses, assumptions, and inputs consistent with those described in the SRP. The NRC staff concluded that the assumptions presented in Table 15.3 and TVA's calculated dose results given in Table 15.1 of this SSER were acceptable. The NRC staff concluded that TVA's estimates of the dose consequences of a design-basis MSLB are in accordance with the SRP acceptance criteria.

### 15.4.3  Steam Generator Tube Rupture

The NRC staff previously reviewed the SGTR radiological dose consequence analysis performed for WBN Units 1 and 2 and documented the results of its review in the SER and in SSERs 3, 5, 12, 14, and 15 (issued June 1995).  Subsequently, the NRC issued WBN Unit1 an operating license, and it began commercial operation in 1996.  Since the initial NRC staff review, TVA made changes to the SGTR radiological dose consequence analysis for Unit 1 using the 10 CFR 50.59 change process and the 10 CFR 50.90 license amendment process.  To complete this SSER, the NRC staff used the CLB SGTR assumptions for Unit 1 as a benchmark for acceptability of the Unit 2 analysis and addressed the following revised Unit 1 parameters and assumptions that are different for Unit 2.

*Steam Release Values*

Unit 2 steam release values are different from Unit 1 values because the Unit 1 steam generators have been replaced by differently designed models.  The Unit 2 secondary-side mass releases from the ruptured and intact steam generator and primary coolant are based on a reactor coolant system (RCS) with the OSGs.

*Iodine Spike Assumptions*

For Unit 2, the short-term maximum allowable DEI value is 14 µCi/gm.  TVA has informed the NRC staff (reference ADAMS Accession No. ML11252A530) that it will submit a license amendment request to revise the Unit 1 TS short-term maximum allowable DEI from 21 µCi/gm to 14 µCi/gm.  This change is necessary since the DCFs were changed from ICRP-2 values to RG 1.109 values.  The Unit 1 TSs require that RG 1.109 be used to determine the DEI.  With this change, the short-term maximum allowable DEI value of 14 µCi/gm will be consistent for both WBN Unit 1 and Unit 2.  The NRC staff has endorsed the use of the DCFs from RG 1.109 in dose consequence analyses.

*Source Term*

The source term used in the SGTR dose consequence analysis performed for Unit 2 differs from the Unit 1 SGTR source term because the Unit 1 source term is based on the failure of two TPBARs, whereas the Unit 2 source term is based on a standard core.  The Unit 2 SGTR dose consequence analysis did not consider TPBARs, since TVA did not request permission to produce tritium in Unit 2.

*Atmospheric Dispersion Factors*

The Unit 2 atmospheric dispersion coefficients are based on the Unit 2 release location at the Unit 2 vent valve stacks and the Unit 2 CR air intake on the east side of the control building.

The NRC staff review concluded that the aforementioned unit-specific changes used to evaluate the WBN Unit 2 SGTR analysis are based on physical differences in the units, unit-specific operational differences, or updated information that has been accepted by the NRC staff for use in dose consequence analyses.  The TVA evaluation concluded that the radiological consequences resulting from the postulated SGTR at the EAB, LPZ, and CR comply with the reference values and the CR dose criterion provided in 10 CFR 100.11 and 10 CFR Part 50,

Appendix A, GDC 19, as well as with the accident-specific dose guidelines specified in the SRP. The NRC staff's review found that TVA used analysis, assumptions, and inputs consistent with those described in the SRP. The NRC staff concluded that the assumptions presented in Table 15.4 and the TVA's calculated dose results given in Table 15.1 of this SSER were acceptable. The NRC staff concludes that TVA's estimates of the dose consequences of a design-basis SGTR are in accordance with the SRP acceptance criteria.

### 15.4.4 Control Rod Ejection Accident

The NRC staff evaluated the control rod ejection accident in Section 15.4.4 of the SER (NUREG-0847), and there have been no supplements to this section. The current WBN Unit 2 FSAR Section 15.5, "Environmental Consequences of Accidents," does not include a detailed evaluation of this accident except to state that it is bounded by the LOCA. The LOCA dose consequence results for WBN Unit 2 are less than 25 percent of the reference values in 10 CFR 100.11. Since the source term for a control rod ejection accident is considerably less than for a LOCA, and the dose consequence results for the WBN Unit 2 LOCA are less than the SRP acceptance criteria for a rod ejection accident (25 percent of the reference values in 10 CFR 100.11), the staff concludes that the dose consequence for the rod ejection accident will be bounded by the LOCA for WBN Unit 2.

### 15.4.5 Fuel-Handling Accident

#### 15.4.5.1    Fuel-Handling Accident, Regulatory Guide 1.25 Analysis

The NRC staff previously reviewed the FHA radiological dose consequence analysis performed for WBN Units 1 and 2 in the SER and in SSERs 4 and 15 (issued June 1995). Subsequently, the NRC issued WBN Unit 1 an operating license, and it began commercial operation in 1996. Since the initial NRC staff review, TVA made changes to the FHA radiological dose consequence analysis for Unit 1 using the 10 CFR 50.59 change process and the 10 CFR 50.90 license amendment process. To complete this SSER, the NRC staff used the CLB FHA assumptions for Unit 1 as a benchmark for acceptability of the Unit 2 analysis and addressed the revised Unit 1 parameters and assumptions that are different for Unit 2.

*Source Term*

In the CLB for the WBN Unit 1 FHA, two TPBARs in the dropped assembly are assumed to break and release the entire contents of tritium. All of the tritium is conservatively assumed to evaporate into the air. The Unit 2 analysis does not consider TPBARs since TVA did not request permission to produce tritium in Unit 2.

In its letter dated September 23, 2011 (ADAMS Accession No. ML11269A064), TVA provided the results of a revised dose consequence analysis for the FHA. The revised analysis includes the following changes to the FHA for Unit 2:

- The damper closure times for auxiliary building and main CR dampers in the normal ventilation system are changed.

- The alternative source term (AST) is used as the basis for the dose calculations for the FHA in the auxiliary building and for the FHA in containment when the equipment hatch is open.

- The meteorology data for the 20-year period of 1991 to 2010 are incorporated, as opposed to the 1976 to 1993 data used for licensing Unit 1.

TVA provided two separate dose consequence analyses covering three cases for the FHA. The first case considered by TVA is for an FHA inside containment with the containment penetrations closed to the auxiliary building and the reactor building purge ventilation system (RBPVS) operating. This case was evaluated using the assumptions from RG 1.25, "Assumptions Used for Evaluating the Potential Radiological Consequences of a Fuel Handling Accident in the Fuel Handling and Storage Facility for Boiling and Pressurized Water Reactors (Safety Guide 25)," issued March 1972, and NUREG-5009, "Assessment of the Use of Extended Burnup Fuel in Light Water Power Reactors," issued February 1989, as reviewed by the NRC staff in the SER and in SSERs 4 and 15. The release is from the shield building vent with credit taken for the RBPVS filtration. A filter efficiency of 90 percent for inorganic iodine and 30 percent for organic iodine for the purge air exhaust filters is used, since no relative humidity control is provided.

The second case considered by the applicant is for an FHA in the spent fuel pool (SFP) area located in the auxiliary building. This case was evaluated using the assumptions from RG 1.183, "Alternative Radiological Source Terms for Evaluating Design Basis Accidents at Nuclear Power Reactors," issued July 2000. In this case, no credit is taken in the analysis for the auxiliary building gas treatment system (ABGTS) or containment purge system filters.

The third case is an open containment case for an FHA inside containment where there is open communication between the containment and the auxiliary building. This evaluation also uses the AST assumptions from RG 1.183 with no credit for any filtration systems.

The NRC staff reviewed the unit-specific changes used to evaluate the RG 1.25 WBN Unit 2 FHA analysis and finds that these changes are based on physical differences in the units, unit-specific operational differences, or updated information that has been accepted by the NRC staff for use in dose consequence analyses. The TVA evaluation concluded that the radiological consequences at the EAB, LPZ, and CR resulting from the postulated FHA inside containment, with the containment closed and the RBPVS operating, comply with the reference values and the CR dose criterion provided in 10 CFR 100.11 and 10 CFR Part 50, Appendix A, GDC 19, as well as with the accident-specific dose guidelines specified in the SRP. The NRC staff's review concluded that TVA used analyses, assumptions, and inputs consistent with those described in the SRP. The NRC staff concluded that the assumptions presented in Table 15.5 and TVA's calculated dose results given in Table 15.1 of this SSER were acceptable. The NRC staff concludes that TVA's estimates of the dose consequences of a design-basis FHA inside containment with the containment isolated and the RBPVS operating are in accordance with the SRP acceptance criteria.

15.4.5.2    Fuel-Handling Accident, Regulatory Guide 1.183, Alternative Source Term Analysis

This accident analysis postulates that a spent fuel assembly is dropped during fuel handling and strikes an adjacent assembly during the fall. All of the fuel rods in the dropped assembly are conservatively assumed to experience fuel cladding damage, releasing the radionuclides within the fuel rod gap to the fuel pool or reactor cavity water. The affected assembly is assumed to contain the maximum inventory of fission products. Volatile constituents of the core fission product inventory migrate from the fuel pellets to the gap between the pellets and the fuel rod clad during normal power operations. The fission product inventory in the fuel rod gap of the damaged fuel rods is assumed to be instantaneously released to the surrounding water as a result of the accident. Fission products released from the damaged fuel are decontaminated by passage through the overlaying water in the reactor cavity or SFP, depending on their physical and chemical form.

TVA provided its analysis of the accident to the staff in a letter dated September 23, 2011. TVA assumed no decontamination for noble gases, a decontamination factor (DF) of 200 for radioiodines, and retention of all particulate fission products. As described in RG 1.183, the FHA is analyzed based on the assumption that 100 percent of the fission products released from the reactor cavity or SFP are released to the environment in 2 hours. TVA conservatively did not credit filtration, holdup, or dilution of the released activity. Since the assumptions and inputs are identical for the FHA within containment and the FHA outside containment, the results of the two events are identical.

TVA considered the analysis of the FHA both within the containment and within the auxiliary building. The dropped fuel assembly inside the containment is assumed to occur with the equipment maintenance hatch fully open, and the fuel assembly drop inside the auxiliary building credits no filtration of the exhaust. A minimum water level of 23 feet above the damaged fuel assembly is maintained for release locations both inside containment and the auxiliary building. This minimum water covering acts as a barrier to many of the radionuclides released from the dropped assembly. TVA assumed retention of all noniodine particulates in the pool, while the iodine releases from the fuel gap into the pool are assumed to be decontaminated by an overall factor of 200. This DF results in 0.5 percent (i.e., 99.5 percent of the iodine is retained in the pool) of the radioiodine escaping the overlying water with a composition of 70-percent elemental and 30-percent organic iodine. In accordance with Regulatory Position 3 of RG 1.183, the applicant assumed that 100 percent of the noble gas activity is released from the pool. All fission products released to the environment are assumed to release over a 2-hour period. In the subject RG 1.183 FHA analysis, TVA does not credit dilution within the surrounding structures before release to the atmosphere. These assumptions follow the guidance of RG 1.183 and are, therefore, acceptable to the staff.

15.4.5.3     Fuel-Handling Accident, Regulatory Guide 1.183 Source Term

TVA provided its analysis of the accident to the staff in a letter dated September 23, 2011. For the purpose of this analysis, TVA assumed a conservative estimate of 100 hours of decay time before any movement of fuel. The core fission product inventory that constitutes the source term for this event is the gap activity in the 264 fuel rods assumed to be damaged as a result of the postulated design-basis FHA. Volatile constituents of the core fission product inventory migrate from the fuel pellets to the gap between the pellets and the fuel rod cladding during normal power operations. The fission product inventory in the fuel rod gap of the damaged fuel rods is assumed to be instantaneously released to the surrounding water as a result of the accident, as in Regulatory Position 1.2 of RG 1.183.

For the FHA occurring inside containment, TVA assumed that the equipment maintenance hatch is open at the time of the accident and that the release from the containment occurs with no credit taken for containment isolation, no credit for dilution or mixing in the containment atmosphere, and no credit for filtration of the released effluent. For the FHA occurring in the auxiliary building, TVA also assumed no credit for filtration of the activity released from the SFP water before it is released to the environment.

As corrected by item 8 of Regulatory Issue Summary 2006-04, "Experience with Implementation of Alternative Source Terms" (ADAMS Accession No. ML053460347), RG 1.183, Appendix B, Regulatory Position 2, should read as follows:

> If the depth of water above the damaged fuel is 23 feet or greater, the decontamination factors for the elemental and organic species are 285 and 1, respectively, giving an overall effective decontamination factor of 200 (i.e., 99.5% of the total iodine released from the damaged rods is retained by the water). This difference in decontamination factors for elemental (99.85%) and organic iodine (0.15%) species results in the iodine above the water being composed of 70% elemental and 30% organic species.

As noted previously, TVA maintains a minimum water depth of 23 feet to cover the underlying damaged fuel assembly in both the reactor cavity and SFP for the FHA analyzed. The assumed 264 damaged fuel rods in the pool release 100 percent of their gap activity within the water, which is scrubbed by the water column as it rises. This scrubbing decontaminates the iodine gap releases with an overall DF of 200. This DF results in 0.5 percent (i.e., 99.5 percent of the iodine is retained in the pool) of the radioiodine escaping the overlying water with a composition of 70-percent elemental and 30-percent organic iodine. Additionally, 100 percent of the noble gas gap activity is assumed to exit the pool, as in Regulatory Position 3 of RG 1.183.

TVA evaluated an FHA in the SFP area and in an open containment with no credit taken for the ABGTS or containment purge system filters and concluded that the radiological consequences at the EAB, outer boundary of the LPZ, and CR are within the reference values and the CR dose criterion provided in 10 CFR 50.67, "Accident Source Term," as well as the accident-specific dose guidelines specified in SRP Section 15.0.1. The staff's review concluded that TVA used analyses, assumptions, and inputs consistent with the regulatory guidance specified in RG 1.183 for the evaluation of an FHA using the AST. The staff concluded that the assumptions by TVA presented in Table 15.6 of this SSER were acceptable. Table 15.1 of this SSER gives TVA's calculated dose results. The staff concludes that the doses estimated by TVA for the WBN Unit 2 FHA will meet the requirements of 10 CFR 50.67 and the guidelines of RG 1.183 and are, therefore, acceptable.

15.4.6 Failure of Small Lines Carrying Coolant outside Containment

The NRC staff previously evaluated the failure of small lines carrying coolant outside containment in Section 15.4.6 of the SER (NUREG-0847). There have been no supplements to this section. The current WBN Unit 2 FSAR Section 15.5, "Environmental Consequences of Accidents," does not include an evaluation of this accident. In the analysis reviewed in the SER, the primary coolant maximum equilibrium fission product concentration was evaluated at 1.0 µCi/gm DEI. The current WBN Unit 2 TS limit for the primary coolant maximum equilibrium fission product concentration of DEI is 0.265 µCi/gm. Therefore, the analysis reviewed in the SER would be bounding for WBN Unit 2.

15.4.7 Environmental Consequences of a Postulated Loss of AC Power to the Plant Auxiliaries

NUREG-0847 does not include an NRC staff review for the radiological dose consequences of a postulated loss of ac power to the plant auxiliaries. For the completion of this SSER, the NRC staff used the CLB assumptions for Unit 1 loss of ac power as a benchmark for acceptability of the Unit 2 analysis and only addressed the following revised Unit 1 parameters and assumptions that are different for Unit 2.

## Source Term

TVA performed a conservative analysis of the potential offsite doses resulting from this accident with steam generator leakage as a parameter. For the Unit 2 analysis, TVA replaced the Unit 1 analysis assumptions of 1-percent defective fuel and a realistic source term with the TS allowable secondary coolant source term of 0.1 µCi/g DEI. In addition, the source terms used in the dose consequence analyses performed for Unit 2 differ from the Unit 1 source terms, because the Unit 1 source terms are based on a tritium core, whereas the Unit 2 source terms are based on a standard core. The Unit 2 dose consequence analysis did not consider TPBARs since TVA did not request permission to produce tritium in Unit 2.

## Steam Release

The volume of steam released in the Unit 1 analysis is based on the use of the replacement steam generators, whereas the volume of steam release in the Unit 2 analysis is based on the use of the OSGs.

## Dose Conversion Factors

For the Unit 2 analysis, TVA incorporated the DCFs from RG 1.109, Appendix E. The NRC staff has endorsed the use of the DCFs from RG 1.109 in dose consequence analyses.

## Atmospheric Dispersion Coefficients

The Unit 2 atmospheric dispersion coefficients are based on a release from the Unit 2 vent valve stacks to the emergency CR intake.

The postulated accidents involving release of steam from the secondary system will not result in a release of radioactivity unless there is leakage from the RCS to the secondary system in the steam generator. TVA presented a conservative analysis of the potential offsite doses resulting from this accident with steam generator leakage as a parameter. This conservative analysis incorporates the TS limit of 0.1 µCi/gm DEI for the secondary coolant. In addition, TVA provided an analysis using a realistic secondary-side source term based on American National Standards Institute/American Nuclear Society (ANSI/ANS)-18.1, "Radioactive Source Term for Normal Operation for Light Water Reactors," issued 1984. TVA used DCFs in ICRP-30, "Limits for Intakes of Radionuclides by Workers," 1979, to determine thyroid doses in place of those found in ICRP-2. Table 15.7 of this SSER lists the parameters used in both the realistic and conservative analyses.

Table 15.1 of this SSER shows TVA's calculated gamma and thyroid doses for the loss of ac power to the plant auxiliaries at the EAB and LPZ for both the realistic and conservative analyses. The doses for this accident are well within the limits of 10 CFR 100.11. Table 15.1 presents TVA's estimated whole body and thyroid dose to CR personnel from the radiation sources discussed above. Table 15.9 of this SSER includes parameters for the CR analysis. The whole body dose is below the 10 CFR Part 50, Appendix A, GDC 19 limit of 5 rem for CR personnel, and the thyroid dose is below the 30-rem acceptance criteria stated in SRP Section 6.4, "Control Room Habitability System," Revision 3, issued March 2007; therefore, they are acceptable.

## 15.4.8 Environmental Consequences of a Postulated Waste Gas Decay Tank Rupture

TVA performed two separate analyses of the postulated waste gas decay tank rupture. The first analysis used realistic assumptions, while the second analysis is based on the assumptions found in RG 1.24, "Assumptions Used for Evaluating the Potential Radiological Consequences of a Pressurized Water Reactor Gas Storage Tank Failure," dated March 23, 1972. Table 15.8 of this SSER lists the parameters used for each of these analyses.

The conservative analysis assumes that the reactor has been operating at full power with 1 percent of the fuel experiencing cladding defects. The realistic analysis assumes that the source term is consistent with ANSI/ANS-18.1-1984 methodology.

Both analyses assume that the tank rupture occurs immediately upon completion of the waste gas transfer, releasing the entire contents of the tank through the auxiliary building vent to the outside atmosphere. The assumption of the release of the noble gas inventory from only a single tank is based on the fact that all gas decay tanks will be isolated from each other whenever they are in use.

Both TVA analyses use conservative assumptions to evaluate the doses from the released activity. TVA used the DCFs in ICRP-30. Table 15.1 of this SSER includes TVA's whole body gamma and thyroid doses for the gas decay tank rupture at the EAB and LPZ and to CR personnel for both the realistic and RG 1.24 analyses. Table 15.9 of this SSER contains the parameters for the CR analysis.

There are no revised Unit 2 parameters for this accident analysis because the waste gas system is common to Units 1 and 2. Therefore, the licensing basis for the proposed Unit 2 analysis is the same as the licensing basis for Unit 1 regarding the environmental consequences of a postulated waste gas decay tank rupture. Since the NRC staff has approved the analysis for Unit 1, it is also acceptable for Unit 2.

## Table 15.1 Radiological Consequences of Design-Basis Accidents

| Postulated accident | EAB rem WB[1]/Thyroid TEDE[2] | LPZ rem WB/Thyroid TEDE | CR rem WB/Thyroid TEDE |
|---|---|---|---|
| Loss of coolant | 2.1E+00/4.0E+01 | 2.2E+00/1.4E+01 | 1.1E+00/3.8E+00 |
| **Steamline break outside secondary containment** | | | |
| Preaccident iodine spike DEI-131 at 14 µCi/gm | 2.7E-02/2.4E+00 | 1.1E-02/1.2E+00 | 4.3E-03/7.4E+00 |
| Accident-initiated iodine spike DEI-131 at 0.265 µCi/gm | 1.0E-01/3.1E+00 | 1.3E-01/4.8E+00 | 8.0E-03/1.0E+01 |
| Control rod ejection | Bounded by the LOCA[3] | | |
| **FHA** | | | |
| In auxiliary building or open containment—RG 1.183 | 2.4E+00 | 6.7E-01 | 1.0E+00 |
| In reactor building, containment closed—RG 1.25 | 4.3E-01/4.2E+01 | 1.2E-01/1.2E+01 | 2.7E-01/6.8E+00 |
| Small line break outside containment | This accident is no longer part of FSAR Section 15.5. | | |
| **SGTR** | | | |
| Preaccident iodine spike DEI-131 at 14 µCi/gm | 3.8E-01/1.4E+01 | 1.1E-01/3.8E+00 | 6.2E-02/1.2E+01 |
| Accident-initiated iodine spike DEI-131 at 0.265 µCi/gm | 5.5E-01/7.2E+00 | 1.6E-01/2.1E+00 | 5.7E-02/2.0E+00 |
| **Loss of ac power** | | | |
| Conservative analysis | 7.5E-04/4.6E-02 | 4.2E-04/2.6E-02 | 2.1E-04/2.1E-02 |
| Realistic analysis | 1.8E-08/1.1E-06 | 1.0E-08/6.2E-07 | 5.1E-09/5.0E-07 |
| **Gas decay tank rupture** | | | |
| RG 1.24 analysis | 6.0E-01/1.3E-02 | 1.7E-01/3.6E-03 | 8.4E-01/7.0E-03 |
| Realistic analysis | 2.9E-02/1.2E-02 | 8.1E-03/3.4E-03 | 3.8E-02/6.5E-03 |

---

[1]     WB is defined as whole body gamma dose.
[2]     TEDE is defined as total effective dose equivalent.
[3]     Note that the WBN Unit 2 LOCA dose is less than 25 percent of the 10 CFR 100.11 limits and, therefore, meets the accident dose criteria for a control rod ejection accident.

| | |
|---|---|
| Power level | 3565 MWt |
| Primary containment free volume | 1.27 E6 ft$^3$ |
| Shield building annulus free volume | 3.75 E5 ft$^3$ |
| Primary containment deck (air return) fan flow rate | 40,000 cfm |
| Number of containment deck air return fans operating | 1 of 2 |
| | |
| Fractions of core inventory available for release | |
|     Noble gases | 100% |
|     Iodines | 25% |
| | |
| Initial iodine composition in containment | |
|     Elemental | 91% |
|     Organic | 4% |
|     Particulate | 5% |
| | |
| Primary containment leak rates | |
|     0–24 hr | 0.25% per day |
|     1–30 days | 0.125% per day |
| Percent of primary containment leakage to auxiliary building | 25% |
| | |
| ABGTS filter efficiencies | |
|     elemental iodine | 99% |
|     methyl iodine | 99% |
|     particulate iodine | 99% |
| | |
| Delay time of activity in auxiliary building before ABGTS operation | None |
| Delay time before filtration credit is taken for the ABGTS | 4 minutes |
| Mean holdup time in auxiliary building after initial 4 minutes | 0.3 hours |
| ABGTS flow rate | 9000 cfm |
| Leakage from auxiliary building to ABGTS downstream HVAC (bypass of filters) | 27.88 cfm |
| | |
| Leakage from ABGTS HVAC into auxiliary building | 8.87 cfm |
| Leakage from auxiliary building into EGTS downstream HVAC (bypass of filters) | 10.7 cfm |
| | |
| Leakage from auxiliary building to environment from single failure of ABGTS (from 30 minutes to 34 minutes post-LOCA) | 9900 cfm (for 4 minutes) |
| | |
| Percent of primary containment leakage to annulus | 75% |
| Percent of annulus free volume available for mixing of recirculated activity | 50% |
| | |
| Number of emergency gas treatment system air-handling units operating | 1 of 2 |

· Table 15.2 (Page 2 of 2)
**Assumptions Used To Calculate the Radiological Consequences Following a Postulated LOCA**

Emergency gas treatment system filter efficiencies

| | |
|---|---|
| elemental iodine | 99% |
| methyl iodine | 99% |
| particulate iodine | 99% |

Shield building mixing model 50% mixing

### Ice Condenser Elemental and Particulate Iodine Removal Efficiency

| Time Interval Post-LOCA (Hours) | Removal Efficiency |
|---|---|
| 0.0 to 0.156 | 0.96 |
| 0.156 to 0.267 | 0.76 |
| 0.267 to 0.323 | 0.73 |
| 0.323 to 0.489 | 0.71 |
| 0.489 to 0.615 | 0.60 |
| 0.615 to 0.768 | 0.58 |
| 0.768 to 0.824 | 0.40 |
| 0.824 to 720 | 0.0 |

### LOCA Atmospheric Dispersion Factors ($\chi$/Q, s/m$^3$)

| Time Period (hr) | CR | | EAB | LPZ |
|---|---|---|---|---|
| | West CR Intake Used in Dose Analysis | East CR Intake Available by Procedure | | |
| 0–2 | 1.09E-03 | | ·6.38E-04 | 1.784E-04 |
| 2–8 | 9.44E-04 | | | 8.835E-05 |
| 8–24 | 1.56E-04 | 1.26E-04 | | 6.217E-05 |
| 24–96 | 1.16E-04 | 9.53E-05 | | 2.900E-05 |
| 96–720 | 9.59E-05 | 8.07E-05 | | 9.811E-06 |

## Table 15.3
## Assumptions Used To Evaluate the Radiological Consequences Following a Postulated MSLB Accident Outside Containment

| | |
|---|---|
| Power level | 3565 MWt |
| Initial maximum RCS equilibrium activity | 0.265 µCi/g |
| Accident-initiated iodine spike appearance rate | 500 times equilibrium rate |
| Maximum preaccident spike iodine concentration | 14.0 µCi/gm |
| Secondary coolant iodine activity | 0.1 µCi/gm DEI |

Primary-to-secondary leak rate
    Faulted steam generator      1.0 gpm
    Per intact steam generator      150 gpd

Steam generator secondary-side iodine partition coefficients
    Faulted steam generator      1 (none)
    Intact steam generator      100

RCS letdown flow rate      124.39 gpm

Steam releases
    Faulted steam generator (0–30 minutes)      96,100 lbm
    Three intact steam generators (0–2 hr)      433,079 lbm
    Three intact steam generators (2–8 hr)      870,754 lbm

MSLB Atmospheric Dispersion Factors ($\chi$/Q, s/m$^3$)

| Time period (hr) | CR | EAB | LPZ |
|---|---|---|---|
| 0–2 | 2.59E-03 | 6.38E-04 | 1.784E-04 |
| 2–8 | 2.12E-03 | | 8.835E-05 |

## Table 15.4
## Assumptions Used To Evaluate the Radiological Consequences Following a Postulated SGTR Accident

Power level                                                   3565 MWt
Initial maximum RCS equilibrium activity                     0.265 µCi/g
Accident-initiated iodine spike appearance rate              500 times equilibrium rate
Maximum pre-accident spike iodine concentration              14.0 µCi/gm
Secondary coolant iodine activity                            ANSI/ANS-18.1-1984
                                                             Expected levels,150 gpd/SG

Primary-to-secondary leak rate
    Faulted steam generator                          1.0 gpm
    Per intact steam generator                       150 gpd

Steam generator secondary-side iodine partition coefficients
    Faulted steam generator                          1 (none)
    Intact steam generator                           100

Secondary-side mass release (ruptured steam generator)
    0–2 hours                                        103,300 lbm
    2–8 hours                                        32,800 lbm
Secondary-side mass release (intact steam generator)
    0–2 hours                                        492,100 lbm
    2–8 hours                                        900,200 lbm

Primary coolant mass release
    Total                                            191,400 lbm
    Flashed                                          10,077.2 lbm

### SGTR Atmospheric Dispersion Factors ($\chi/Q$, s/m$^3$)

| Time period (hr) | CR | EAB | LPZ |
|---|---|---|---|
| 0–2 | 2.59E-03 | 6.38E-04 | 1.784E-04 |
| 2–8 | 2.12E-03 | | 8.835E-05 |

## Table 15.5
## Assumptions Used To Evaluate the Radiological Consequences Following a Postulated FHA Inside Closed Containment—RG 1.25 Analysis

| | |
|---|---|
| Core thermal power level | 3565 MWt |
| Radial peaking factor | 1.65 |
| Number of fuel assemblies in the core | 193 |
| Fuel rods per assembly | 264 |
| Core average assembly power | 18.47 MWth |
| Number of fuel assemblies damaged | 1 (all rods ruptured) |
| Minimum postshutdown fuel-handling time (decay time) | 100 hours |
| | |
| Minimum pool water depth | 23 feet |

Fuel clad damage gap release fractions

| | |
|---|---|
| I-131 | 12% |
| Remainder of halogens | 10% |
| Kr-85 | 14% |
| Xe-133 | 5% |
| Xe-135 | 2% |
| Remainder of noble gases | 10% |

Pool DF

| | |
|---|---|
| Noble gases and organic iodine | 1 |
| Aerosols | Infinite |
| Elemental iodine (23 ft of water cover) | 133 |
| Overall iodine (23 ft of water cover) | 200 (effective DF) |

Chemical form of iodine released

| | |
|---|---|
| Elemental | 99.75% |
| Organic | 0.25% |

RBPVS — Filter efficiencies auxiliary building

| | |
|---|---|
| Elemental iodine | 90% |
| Organic iodine | 30% |

| | |
|---|---|
| Duration of release to the environment | 2-hour release |

### FHA Atmospheric Dispersion Factors ($\chi/Q$, s/m$^3$)

| Time period (hr) | CR | EAB | LPZ |
|---|---|---|---|
| 0–2 | 2.59E-03 | 6.38E-04 | 1.784E-04 |

## Table 15.6
### Assumptions Used To Evaluate the Radiological Consequences Following a Postulated FHA in the Auxiliary Building or in Open Containment—RG 1.183 Analysis

| | |
|---|---|
| Core thermal power level | 3565 MWt |
| Radial peaking factor | 1.65 |
| Number of fuel assemblies in the core | 193 |
| Fuel rods per assembly | 264 |
| Core average assembly power | 18.47 MWth |
| | |
| Number of fuel assemblies damaged | 1 (all rods ruptured) |
| Minimum postshutdown fuel-handling time (decay time) | 100 hours |
| | |
| Minimum pool water depth | 23 feet |

Fuel clad damage gap release fractions

| | |
|---|---|
| I-131 | 8% |
| Remainder of halogens | 5% |
| Kr-85 | 10% |
| Remainder of noble gases | 5% |

Pool DF

| | |
|---|---|
| Noble gases and organic iodine | 1 |
| Aerosols | Infinite |
| Elemental iodine (23 ft of water cover) | 285 |
| Overall iodine (23 ft of water cover) | 200 (effective DF) |

Chemical form of iodine released

| | |
|---|---|
| Elemental | 99.85% |
| Organic | 0.15% |
| | |
| Filter efficiencies | None |
| | |
| Duration of release to the environment | 2-hour release |

### FHA Atmospheric Dispersion Factors ($\chi$/Q, s/m$^3$)

| Time period (hr) | CR | EAB | LPZ |
|---|---|---|---|
| 0–2 | 2.59E-03 | 6.38E-04 | 1.784E-04 |

## Table 15.7
## Assumptions Used To Evaluate the Radiological Consequences Following a Postulated Loss of AC Power to the Plant Auxiliaries

Core thermal power level                          3565 MWt

Steam generator tube leak rate                    1 gpm

Fuel defects (clad damage)
    Realistic analysis                            ANSI/ANS 18.1-1984
    Conservative analysis                         0.1 µCi/gm DEI

Iodine partition factor                           0.01

Blowdown rate                                     25 gpm per steam generator

Duration of plant cooldown                        8 hours

Steam release (total)
    0–2 hours                                     444,875 lbm
    2–8 hours                                     903,530 lbm

### Loss of AC Power Atmospheric Dispersion Factors ($\chi/Q$, s/m$^3$)

| Time period (hr) | CR | EAB | LPZ |
|---|---|---|---|
| 0–2 | 2.59E-03 | 6.38E-04 | 1.784E-04 |

**Table 15.8**
**Assumptions Used To Evaluate the Radiological Consequences Following a Postulated Waste Gas Decay Tank Rupture**

| | |
|---|---|
| Core thermal power level | 3565 MWt |

Steam generator tube leak rate      1 gpm

Fuel defects (clad damage)
    Realistic analysis                              ANSI/ANS-18.1-1984
    Conservative analysis RG 1.24        1%

Activity released from GWPS[4]

    Realistic analysis                              Maximum isotopic concentrations and actual plant flow rates

| | |
|---|---|
| Conservative analysis RG 1.24 | Selected isotopes (Curies) |
| Xe-131m | 8.9E+02 |
| Xe-133 | 6.8E+04 |
| Xe-133m | 1.0E+03 |
| Xe-135 | 9.4E+02 |
| Kr-85 | 4.2E+03 |
| Kr-85m | 1.3E+02 |
| I-131 | 4.8E-02 |

Time of accident
    Realistic analysis                              After tank fill
    Conservative analysis RG 1.24        End of equilibrium core cycle

Waste Gas Decay Tank Rupture Atmospheric Dispersion Factors ($\chi/Q$, s/m$^3$)

| Time period (hr) | CR | EAB | LPZ |
|---|---|---|---|
| 0–2 | 2.56E-03 | 6.38E-04 | 1.784E-04 |

---

[4]      GWPS is defined as gaseous waste processing system.

**Table 15.9**
**CR Parameters**

| | |
|---|---|
| Volume | 257,198 cu ft |
| Makeup/pressurization flow | 711 cfm |
| Recirculation flow | 2889 cfm |
| Unfiltered intake | 51 cfm |
| Filter efficiency | |
|     First pass | 95% |
|     Second pass | 70% |
| Isolation time | 40 seconds |
| Occupancy factors | |
|     0–24 hours | 100% |
|     1–4 days | 60% |
|     4–30 days | 40% |

# APPENDIX A

## CHRONOLOGY OF RADIOLOGICAL REVIEW OF
## WATTS BAR NUCLEAR PLANT, UNIT 2, OPERATING LICENSE REVIEW

Public correspondence exchanged between the NRC and TVA during the review of the operating license application for Watts Bar Nuclear Plant (WBN), Units 1 and 2, is available through the NRC's Agencywide Documents Access and Management System (ADAMS) or the Public Document Room (PDR). This correspondence includes that occurring subsequent to TVA's letter notifying the NRC of its decision to reactivate construction of WBN Unit 2, which had been in a deferred status under the Commission's Policy Statement on Deferred Plants.

Web-based ADAMS (WBA) is the latest interface to ADAMS. This search engine enables searching the ADAMS repository of official agency records (Publicly Available Records System (PARS) and Public Legacy libraries) for publicly available regulatory guides, NUREG-series reports, inspection reports, Commission documents, correspondence, and other regulatory and technical documents written by NRC staff, contractors, and licensees. WBA permits full-text searching and enables users to view document images, download files, and print locally. New documents become accessible on the day they are published, and are released periodically throughout the day. ADAMS documents are provided in Adobe Portable Document Format (PDF).

The NRC PDR reference staff is available to assist with ADAMS. Contact information for the PDR staff is on the NRC Web site at http://www.nrc.gov/reading-rm/contact-pdr.html.

# APPENDIX E

## PRINCIPAL CONTRIBUTORS TO SSER 25

D. Allsopp, NRR/DIRS/IOLB
R. Alvarado, NRR/DE/EICB
L. Brown, NRR/DRA/AADB
N. Carte, NRR/DE/EICB
F. Lyon, NRR/DORL/LPWB
P. Milano, NRR/DORL/LPWB
J. Parillo, NRR/DRA/AADB
J. Poehler, NRR/DE/EVIB
J. Poole, NRR/DORL/LPWB
L. Raghavan, NRR/DORL/LPWB

# APPENDIX HH

## WATTS BAR UNIT 2 ACTION ITEMS TABLE

This table provides a status of required action items associated of all open items, confirmatory issues, and proposed license conditions that the staff has identified. Unless otherwise noted, the item references are to sections of this SSER. Items that are still open are listed first, and items that have been closed are listed second. Some numbers were not used in the sequential list. There are **83 items** still open and **41 items** that have been closed as of November 7, 2011.

| Open Items | | | | |
|---|---|---|---|---|
| **Item** | **Type** | **Action Required** | **Lead** | **Status** |
| (1) | CI | Review evaluations and corrective actions associated with a power assisted cable pull. (NRC safety evaluation dated August 31, 2009, ADAMS Accession No. ML092151155) | NRR | Open |
| (2) | CI | Conduct appropriate inspection activities to verify cable lengths used in calculations and analysis match as-installed configuration. (NRC safety evaluation dated August 31, 2009, ADAMS Accession No. ML092151155) | RII | Open |
| (4) | CI | Conduct appropriate inspection activities to verify that TVA's maximum SWBP criteria for signal level and coaxial cables do not exceed the cable manufacturers maximum SWBP criteria. (NRC safety evaluation dated August 31, 2009, ADAMS Accession No. ML092151155) | RII | Open |
| (5) | CI | Verify timely submittal of pre-startup core map and perform technical review. (TVA letter dated September 7, 2007, ADAMS Accession No. ML072570676) | NRR | Open |
| (6) | CI | Verify implementation of TSTF-449. (TVA letter dated September 7, 2007, ADAMS Accession No. ML072570676) | NRR | Open |
| (7) | CI | Verify commitment completion and review electrical design calculations. (TVA letter dated October 9, 1990, ADAMS Accession No. ML073551056) | RII | Open |
| (8) | CI | TVA should provide a pre-startup map to the NRC staff indicating the rodded fuel assemblies and a projected end of cycle burnup of each rodded assembly for the initial fuel cycle 6-months prior to fuel load. (NRC safety evaluation dated May 3, 2010, ADAMS Accession No. ML101200035) | NRR | Open |
| (9) | CI | Confirm that education and experience of management and principal supervisory positions down through the shift supervisory level conform to Regulatory Guide 1.8. (SSER 22, Section 13.1.3) | RII | Open |

| (10) | CI | Confirm that TVA has an adequate number of licensed and non-licensed operators in the training pipeline to support the preoperational test program, fuel loading, and dual unit operation. (SSER 22, Section 13.1.3) | RII | Open |
|------|-----|---|------|------|
| (12) | | TVA's implementation of NGDC PP-20 and EDCR Appendix J is subject to future NRC audit and inspection. (SSER 22, Section 25.9) | NRR | Open |
| (13) | | TVA is expected to submit an IST program and specific relief requests for WBN Unit 2 nine months before the projected date of OL issuance. (SSER 22, Section 3.9.6) | NRR | Open |
| (16) | | Based on the uniqueness of EQ, the NRC staff must perform a detailed inspection and evaluation prior to fuel load to determine how the WBN Unit 2 EQ program complies with the requirements of 10 CFR 50.49. (SSER 22, Section 3.11.2) | RII/NRR | Open |
| (17) | | The NRC staff should verify the accuracy of the WBN Unit 2 EQ list prior to fuel load. (SSER 22, Section 3.11.2.1) | RII/NRR | Open |
| (23) | CI | Resolve whether or not TVA's reasoning for not upgrading the MSIV solenoid valves to Category I is a sound reason to the contrary, as specified in 10 CFR 50.49(l). (SSER 22, Section 3.11.2.2.1; SSER 24, Section 8.1) | NRR | Open |
| (25) | | Prior to the issuance of an operating license, TVA is required to provide satisfactory documentation that it has obtained the maximum secondary liability insurance coverage pursuant to 10 CFR 140.11(a)(4), and not less than the amount required by 10 CFR 50.54(w) with respect to property insurance, and the NRC staff has reviewed and approved the documentation. (SSER 22, Section 22.3) | NRR | Open |
| (26) | | For the scenario with an accident in one unit and concurrent shutdown of the second unit without offsite power, TVA stated that Unit 2 pre-operational testing will validate the diesel response to sequencing of loads on the Unit 2 emergency diesel generators (EDGs). The NRC staff will evaluate the status of this issue and will update the status of the EDG load response in a future SSER. (SSER 22, Section 8.1) | NRR | Open |
| (30) | | TVA should confirm that all other safety-related equipment (in addition to the Class 1E motors) will have adequate starting and running voltage at the most limiting safety related components (such as motor operated valves, contactors, solenoid valves or relays) at the degraded voltage relay setpoint | RII/NRR | Open |

| | | dropout setting. TVA should also confirm that the final Technical Specifications are properly derived from these analytical values for the degraded voltage settings. (SSER 22, Section 8.3.1.2) | | |
|---|---|---|---|---|
| (32) | | TVA should provide to the NRC staff the details of the administrative limits of EDG voltage and speed range, and the basis for its conclusion that the impact is negligible, and describe how it accounts for the administrative limits in the Technical Specification surveillance requirements for EDG voltage and frequency. (SSER 22, Section 8.3.1.14) | NRR | Open |
| (33) | CI | TVA stated in Attachment 9 of its letter dated July 31, 2010, that certain design change notices (DCNs) are required or anticipated for completion of WBN Unit 2, and that these DCNs were unverified assumptions used in its analysis of the 125 Vdc vital battery system. Verification of completion of these DCNs to the NRC staff is necessary prior to issuance of the operating license. (SSER 22, Section 8.3.2.3; SSER 24, Section 8.1) | RII/NRR | Open |
| (35) | | TVA should provide information to the NRC staff that the CCS will produce feedwater purity in accordance with BTP MTEB 5-3 or, alternatively, provide justification for producing feedwater purity to another acceptable standard. (SSER 22, Section 10.4.6) | NRR | Open |
| (37) | CI | The NRC staff will review the combined WBN Unit 1 and 2 Appendix C prior to issuance of the Unit 2 OL to confirm (1) that the proposed Unit 2 changes were incorporated into Appendix C, and (2) that changes made to Appendix C for Unit 1 since Revision 92 and the changes made to the NP-REP since Revision 92 do not affect the bases of the staff's findings in this SER supplement. (SSER 22, Section 13.3.2) | NSIR | Open |
| (38) | CI | The NRC staff will confirm the availability and operability of the ERDS for Unit 2 prior to issuance of the Unit 2 OL. (SSER 22, Section 13.3.2.6) | RII/NSIR | Open |
| (39) | CI | The NRC staff will confirm the adequacy of the communications capability to support dual unit operations prior to issuance of the Unit 2 OL. (SSER 22, Section 13.3.2.6) | RII/NSIR | Open |
| (40) | CI | The NRC staff will confirm the adequacy of the emergency facilities and equipment to support dual unit operations prior to issuance of the Unit 2 OL. (SSER 22, Section 13.3.2.8) | RII/NSIR | Open |
| (41) | CI | TVA committed to (1) update plant data displays as necessary to include Unit 2, and (2) to update dose assessment models to provide capabilities for assessing releases from both WBN units. The NRC | RII/NSIR | Open |

| | | staff will confirm the adequacy of these items prior to issuance of the Unit 2 OL. (SSER 22, Section 13.3.2.9) | | |
|---|---|---|---|---|
| (42) | CI | The NRC staff will confirm the adequacy of the accident assessment capabilities to support dual unit operations prior to issuance of the Unit 2 OL. (SSER 22, Section 13.3.2.9) | RII/NSIR | Open |
| (43) | CI | Section V of Appendix E to 10 CFR Part 50 requires TVA to submit its detailed implementing procedures for its emergency plan no less than 180 days before the scheduled issuance of an operating license. Completion of this requirement will be confirmed by the NRC staff prior to the issuance of an operating license. (SSER 22, Section 13.3.2.18) | NSIR | Open |
| (47) | | The NRC staff noted that TVA's changes to Section 6.2.6 in FSAR Amendment 97, regarding the implementation of Option B of Appendix J, were incomplete, because several statements remained regarding performing water-sealed valve leakage tests "as specified in 10 CFR [Part] 50, Appendix J." With the adoption of Option B, the specified testing requirements are no longer applicable; Option A to Appendix J retains these requirements. The NRC discussed this discrepancy with TVA in a telephone conference on September 28, 2010. TVA stated that it would remove the inaccurate reference to Appendix J for specific water testing requirements in a future FSAR amendment. (SSER 22, Section 6.2.6) | NRR | Open |
| (48) | CI | The NRC staff should verify that its conclusions in the review of FSAR Section 15.4.1 do not affect the conclusions of the staff regarding the acceptability of Section 6.5.3. (SSER 22, Section 6.5.3) | NRR | Open |
| (49) | CI | The NRC staff was unable to determine how TVA linked the training qualification requirements of ANSI N45.2-1971 to TVA Procedure TI-119. Therefore, the implementation of training and qualification for inspectors will be the subject of future NRC staff inspections. (NRC letter dated July 2, 2010, ADAMS Accession No. ML101720050) | RII | Open |
| (50) | CI | TVA stated that about 5 percent of the anchor bolts for safety-related pipe supports do not have quality control documentation, because the pull tests have not yet been performed. Since the documentation is still under development, the NRC staff will conduct inspections to follow-up on the adequate implementation of this construction refurbishment program requirement. (NRC letter dated July 2, 2010, ADAMS Accession No. ML101720050) | RII | Open |

| (51) | CI | The implementation of TVA Procedure TI-119 will be the subject of NRC follow-up inspection to determine if the construction refurbishment program requirements are being adequately implemented. (NRC letter dated July 2, 2010, ADAMS Accession No. ML101720050) | RII | Open |
|---|---|---|---|---|
| (52) through (58) | | Not used. | | |
| (59) | | The staff's evaluation of the compatibility of the ESF system materials with containment sprays and core cooling water in the event of a LOCA is incomplete pending resolution of GSI-191 for WBN Unit 2. (SSER 23, Section 6.1.1.4) | NRR | Open |
| (60) | CI | TVA should amend the FSAR description of the design and operation of the spent fuel pool cooling and cleanup system in FSAR Section 9.1.3 as proposed in its December 21, 2010, letter to the NRC. (SSER 23, Section 9.1.3) | NRR | Open |
| (61) | | TVA should provide information to the NRC staff to demonstrate that PAD 4.0 can conservatively calculate the fuel temperature and other impacted variables, such as stored energy, given the lack of a fuel thermal conductivity degradation model. (SSER 23, Section 4.2.2) | NRR | Open |
| (63) | CI | TVA should confirm to the NRC staff that testing prior to Unit 2 fuel load has demonstrated that two-way communications is impossible with the Eagle 21 communications interface. (SSER 23, Section 7.2.1.1) | RII | Open |
| (64) | CI | TVA stated that, "Post modification testing will be performed to verify that the design change corrects the Eagle 21, Rack 2 RTD accuracy issue prior to WBN Unit 2 fuel load." This issue is open pending NRC staff review of the testing results. (SSER 23, Section 7.2.1.1) | RII | Open |
| (65) | | TVA should provide justification to the staff regarding why different revisions of WCAP-13869 are referenced in WBN Unit 1 and Unit 2. (SSER 23, Section 7.2.1.1) | NRR | Open |
| (66) | CI | TVA should clarify FSAR Section 9.2.5 to add the capability of the UHS to bring the nonaccident unit to cold shutdown within 72 hours. (SSER 23, Section 9.2.5) | NRR | Open |
| (67) | CI | TVA should confirm, and the NRC staff should verify, that the component cooling booster pumps for Unit 2 are above PMF level. (SSER 23, Section 9.2.2) | RII | Open |

| (68) | | Not used. | | |
|------|------|-----------|------|------|
| (69) | CI | The WBN Unit 2 RCS vent system is acceptable, pending verification that the RCS vent system is installed. (SSER 23, Section 5.4.5) | RII | Open |
| (70) | | TVA should provide the revised WBN Unit 2 PSI program ASME Class 1, 2, and 3 Supports "Summary Tables," to include numbers of components so that the NRC staff can verify that the numbers meet the reference ASME Code. (Section 3.2.3 of Appendix Z of SSER 23) | NRR | Open |
| (71) | | By letter dated April 21, 2011 (ADAMS Accession No. ML111110513), TVA withdrew its commitment to replace the Unit 2 clevis insert bolts. TVA should provide further justification for the decision to not replace the bolts to the NRC staff. (SSER 23, Section 3.9.5) | NRR | Open |
| (73) | CI | The NRC staff will inspect to confirm that TVA has completed the WBN Unit 2 EOPs prior to fuel load. (SSER 23, Section 7.5.3) | RII | Open |
| (74) | CI | The NRC staff will verify installation of the acoustic-monitoring system for the power-operated relief valve (PORV) position indication in WBN Unit 2 before fuel load. (SSER 23, Section 7.8.1) | RII | Open |
| (75) | CI | The NRC staff will verify that the test procedures and qualification testing for auxiliary feedwater initiation and control and flow indication are completed in WBN Unit 2 before fuel load. (SSER 23, Section 7.8.2) | RII | Open |
| (77) | | It is unclear to the NRC staff which software V&V documents are applicable to the HRCAR monitors. TVA should clarify which software V&V documents are applicable, in order for the staff to complete its evaluation. (SSER 23, Section 7.5.2.3) | NRR | Open |
| (79) | | TVA should perform a radiated susceptibility survey, after the installation of the hardware but prior to the RM-1000 being placed in service, to establish the need for exclusion distance for the HRCAR monitors while using handheld portable devices (e.g., walkie-talkie) in the control room, as documented in Attachment 23 to TVA's letter dated February 25, 2011, and item number 355 of TVA's letter dated April 15, 2011. (SSER 23, Section 7.5.2.3) | NRR | Open |
| (80) | | TVA should provide clarification to the staff on how TVA Standard Specification SS-E18-14.1 meets the guidance of RG 1.180, and should address any deviations from the guidance of the RG. (SSER 23, Section 7.5.2.3) | NRR | Open |

| (81) | | The extent to which TVA's supplier, General Atomics (GA), complies with EPRI TR-106439 and the methods that GA used for its commercial dedication process should be provided by TVA to the NRC staff for review. (SSER 23, Section 7.5.2.3) | NRR | Open |
|---|---|---|---|---|
| (83) | CI | TVA should confirm to the NRC staff the completion of the data storm test on the DCS. (SSER 23, Section 7.7.1.4) | NRR | Open |
| (84) through (89) | | Not used. | | |
| (90) | CI | The NRC staff should verify that the ERCW dual unit flow balance confirms that the ERCW pumps meet all specified performance requirements and have sufficient capability to supply all required ERCW normal and accident flows for dual unit operation and accident response, in order to verify that the ERCW pumps meet GDC 5 requirements for two-unit operation. (SSER 23, Section 9.2.1) | RII/NRR | Open |
| (91) | | TVA should update the FSAR with information describing how WBN Unit 2 meets GDC 5, assuming the worst case single failure and a LOOP, as provided in TVA's letter dated April 13, 2011. (SSER 23, Section 9.2.1) | NRR | Open |
| (92) | | Not used. | | |
| (93) | | TVA should confirm to the staff that testing of the Eagle 21 system has sufficiently demonstrated that two-way communication to the ICS is precluded with the described configurations. (SSER 23, Section 7.9.3.2) | RII | Open |
| (94) | | TVA should provide to the staff either information that demonstrates that the WBN Unit 2 Common Q PAMS meets the applicable requirements in IEEE Std. 603-1991, or justification for why the Common Q PAMS should not meet those requirements. (SSER 23, Section 7.5.2.2.3) | NRR | Open |
| (98) | | TVA should demonstrate that the WBN Unit 2 Common Q PAMS is in conformance with RG 1.152, Revision 2, or provide justification for not conforming. (SSER 23, Section 7.5.2.2.3) | NRR | Open |
| (101) | | TVA should demonstrate that the WBN Unit 2 Common Q PAMS application software is in conformance with RG 1.168, Revision 1, or provide justification for not conforming. (SSER 23, Section 7.5.2.2.3) | NRR | Open |

| (105) | | TVA should produce an acceptable description of how the WBN Unit 2 Common Q PAMS SysRS and SRS implement the design basis requirements of IEEE Std. 603-1991 Clause 4. (SSER 23, Section 7.5.2.2.3.4.3.1) | NRR | Open |
|---|---|---|---|---|
| (108) | | TVA should demonstrate to the NRC staff that there are no synergistic effects between temperature and humidity for the Common Q PAMS equipment. (SSER 23, Section 7.5.2.2.3.5.2) | NRR | Open |
| (110) | | TVA should provide information to the NRC staff describing how the WBN Unit 2 Common Q PAMS design supports periodic testing of the RVLIS function. (SSER 23, Section 7.5.2.2.3.9.2.6) | NRR | Open |
| (111) | | TVA should confirm to the staff that there are no changes required to the technical specifications as a result of the modification installing the Common Q PAMS. If any changes to the technical specifications are required, TVA should provide the changes to the NRC staff for review. (SSER 23, Section 7.5.2.2.3.11) | NRR | Open |
| (112) | CI | TVA should provide an update to the FSAR reflecting the radiation protection design features descriptive information provided in its letter dated October 4, 2010. (SSER 24, Section 12.4) | NRR | Open |
| (113) | CI | TVA should provide an update to the FSAR reflecting the justification for the periodicity of the COT frequency for WBN non-safety related area radiation monitors. (SSER 24, Section 12.4) | NRR | Open |
| (114) | CI | TVA should update the FSAR to reflect that WBN meets the radiation monitoring requirements of 10 CFR 50.68. (SSER 24, Section 12.4) | NRR | Open |
| (115) | CI | TVA should update the FSAR to reflect the information regarding design changes to be implemented to lower radiation levels as provided in its letter the NRC dated June 3, 2010. (SSER 24, Section 12.5) | NRR | Open |
| (116) | CI | TVA should update the FSAR to reflect the qualification standards of the RPM as provided in its letter to the NRC dated October 4, 2010. (SSER 24, Section 12.6) | NRR | Open |
| (117) | CI | TVA should update the FSAR to reflect the calculational basis for access to vital areas as provided in its letter dated February 25, 2011. (SSER 24, Section 12.7.1) | NRR | Open |
| (118) | | TVA should provide to the NRC staff a description of how the other vanadium detectors within the IITA would be operable following the failure of an SPND. (SSER 24, Section 7.7.1.9.2) | NRR | Open |

| (120) | | TVA must confirm to the NRC staff that the maximum over-voltage or surge voltage that could affect the system is 264 VAC, assuming that the power supply cable to the SPS cabinet is not routed with other cables greater than 264 VAC.  (SSER 24, Section 7.7.1.9.5; SSER 25, Section 7.7.1.9) | NRR | Open |
|-------|--|-----------------------------------------------------------------------------------------------------------------------------------------------------------------------------------------------------------------------------------------------------------------------------------------------|-----|------|
| (121) | | TVA should submit the results to the NRC staff of a 600 VDC dielectric strength test performed on the IITA assembly.  (SSER 24, Section 7.7.1.9.5) | NRR | Open |
| (123) | | TVA should provide an explanation to the NRC staff of how the system will assign a data quality value to notify the power distribution calculation software to disregard data from a failed SPND.  (SSER 24, Section 7.7.1.9.5) | NRR | Open |
| (125) | | TVA should provide clarification to the NRC staff of the type of connector used with the MI cable in Unit 2, and which EQ test is applicable.  (SSER 24, Section 7.7.1.9.5) | NRR | Open |
| (126) | | To enable the NRC staff to evaluate and review the IITA environmental qualification, TVA should provide the summary report of the environmental qualification for the IITA. (SSER 24, Section 7.7.1.9.5) | NRR | Open |
| (127) | | TVA should provide a summary to the NRC staff of the electro-magnetic interference/radio-frequency interference (EMI/RFI) testing for the MI cable electro-magnetic compatibility (EMC) qualification test results.  (SSER 24, Section 7.7.1.9.5) | NRR | Open |
| (129) | | TVA should verify to the NRC staff resolution of the open item in WNA-CN-00157-WBT for the Quint power supply (to be installed in the SPS cabinet) to undergo EMC testing of 4 kV to validate the assumptions made in the Westinghouse analysis. (SSER 24, Section 7.7.1.9.5) | NRR | Open |
| (131) | | TVA should review the EOP action level setpoint to account for the difference between core exit temperature readings for Unit 1 and Unit 2 and confirm the EOP action level setpoint to the NRC staff.  (SSER 24, Section 7.7.1.9.5) | NRR | Open |
| (132) | | TVA must provide the NRC staff with analyses of the boron dilution event that meet the criteria of SRP Section 15.4.6, including a description of the methods and procedures used by the operators to identify the dilution path(s) and terminate the dilution, in order for the staff to determine that the analyses comply with GDC 10.  (SSER 24, Section 15.2.4.4) | NRR | Open |
| (133) | | In order to confirm the stability analysis of the sand baskets used by TVA in the WBN Unit 2 licensing basis, TVA will perform either a hydrology analysis | NRR | Open |

| | | | | |
|---|---|---|---|---|
| | | without crediting the use of the sand baskets at the Fort Loudoun dam for the seismic dam failure and flood combination, or TVA will perform a seismic test of the sand baskets, as stated in TVA's letter dated April 20, 2011.  TVA will report the results of this analysis or test to the NRC by October 31, 2011.  (SSER 24, Section 2.4.10) | | |
| (134) | | TVA should provide to the NRC staff supporting technical justification for the statements in Amendment 104 of FSAR Section 2.4.4.1, "Dam Failure Permutations," page 2.4-32 (in the section "Multiple Failures") that, "Fort Loudoun, Tellico, and Watts Bar have previously been judged not to fail for the OBE (0.09 g).  Postulation of Tellico failure in this combination has not been evaluated but is bounded by the SSE failure of Norris, Cherokee, Douglas and Tellico."  (SSER 24, Section 2.4.10) | NRR | Open |
| (136) | CI | The JFD summary for the data from 1991 through 2010 provided by letter dated November 7, 2011, and a discussion of the long-term representativeness of these data should be provided in the WBN Unit 2 FSAR.  Upon receipt of the updated FSAR, the NRC staff will confirm that these updates have been made by TVA.  (SSER 25, Section 2.3.3) | NRR | Open |
| (137) | CI | The NRC staff will confirm, upon receipt, that TVA integrated the updated CR χ/Q values from its letter dated September 15, 2011, into a future amendment of the FSAR.  (SSER 25, Section 2.3.4) | NRR | Open |
| (138) | CI | Upon receipt of the updated ODCM, the NRC staff will confirm that corresponding revisions related to the updated annual average χ/Q and D/Q values have been made to the ODCM.  (SSER 25, Section 2.3.5) | NRR | Open |
| (139) | CI | The results of the cost-benefit analysis required by 10 CFR Part 50, Appendix I, subsection II.D, should be provided in the WBN Unit 2 FSAR.  Upon receipt of the updated FSAR, the NRC staff will confirm that the update has been made by TVA.  (SSER 25, Section 11.3) | NRR | Open |

| | | | | |
|---|---|---|---|---|
| **Closed Items** | | | | |
| (3) | CI | Confirm TVA submitted update to FSAR section 8.3.1.4.1. (NRC safety evaluation dated August 31, 2009, ADAMS Accession No. ML092151155) Closed in SSER 24, Section 8.1. | NRR | Closed |

| (11) | CI | The plant administrative procedures should clearly state that, when the Assistant Shift Engineer assumes his duties as Fire Brigade Leader, his control room duties are temporarily assumed by the Shift Supervisor (Shift Engineer), or by another SRO, if one is available. The plant administrative procedures should clearly describe this transfer of control room duties. (SSER 22, Section 13.1.3) Closed in SSER 25, Section 13.1.3. | NRR | Closed |
|------|----|------------------------------------------------------------------|------|--------|
| (14) |    | TVA stated that the Unit 2 PTLR is included in the Unit 2 System Description for the Reactor Coolant System (WBN2-68-4001), which will be revised to reflect required revisions to the PTLR by September 17, 2010. (SSER 22, Section 5.3.1) Closed in SSER 25, Section 5.3.1. | NRR | Closed |
| (15) |    | TVA should confirm to the NRC staff the completion of Primary Stress Corrosion Cracking (PWSCC) mitigation activities on the Alloy 600 dissimilar metal butt welds (DMBWs) in the primary loop piping. (SSER 22, Section 3.6.3) Closed in SSER 24, Section 3.6.3. | NRR | Closed |
| (18) |    | Based on the extensive layup period of equipment within WBN Unit 2, the NRC staff must review, prior to fuel load, the assumptions used by TVA to re-establish a baseline for the qualified life of equipment. The purpose of the staff's review is to ensure that TVA has addressed the effects of environmental conditions on equipment during the layup period. (SSER 22, Section 3.11.2.2) Closed in Inspection Report 0500391/2011604, dated June 29, 2011, ADAMS Accession No. ML111810890. | RII/NRR | Closed |
| (19) |    | The NRC staff should complete its review of TVA's EQ Program procedures for WBN Unit 2 prior to fuel load. (SSER 22, Section 3.11.2.2.1) Closed in Inspection Report 0500391/2011604, dated June 29, 2011, ADAMS Accession No. ML111810890. | RII/NRR | Closed |
| (20) | CI | Resolve whether or not routine maintenance activities should result in increasing the EQ of the 6.9 kV motors to Category I status in accordance with 10 CFR 50.49. (SSER 22, Section 3.11.2.2.1; SSER 24, Section 8.1) Closed in Inspection Report 0500391/2011605, dated August 5, 2011, ADAMS Accession No. ML112201418. | RII/NRR | Closed |
| (21) |    | The NRC staff should confirm that the Electrical Penetration Assemblies (EPAs) are installed in the tested configuration, and that the feedthrough module is manufactured by the same company and is consistent with the EQ test report for the EPA. (SSER 22, Section 3.11.2.2.1) Closed in Inspection Report 05000391/2011607, dated September 30, | RII/NRR | Closed |

| | | 2011, ADAMS Accession No. ML112730197. | | |
|---|---|---|---|---|
| (22) | | TVA must clarify its use of the term "equivalent" (e.g., identical, similar) regarding the replacement terminal blocks to the NRC staff. If the blocks are similar, then a similarity analysis should be completed and presented to the NRC for review. (SSER 22, Section 3.11.2.2.1) Closed in SSER 24, Section 8.1. | NRR | Closed |
| (24) | | The NRC staff requires supporting documentation from TVA to justify its establishment of a mild environment threshold for total integrated dose of less than 1x103 rads for electronic components such as semiconductors or electronic components containing organic material. (SSER 22, Section 3.11.2.2.1) Closed in SSER 24, Section 8.1. | NRR | Closed |
| (27) | | TVA should provide a summary of margin studies based on scenarios described in Section 8.1 for CSSTs A, B, C, and D. (SSER 22, Section 8.2.2) Closed in SSER 24, Section 8.1. | NRR | Closed |
| (28) | | TVA should provide to the NRC staff a detailed discussion showing that the load tap changer is able to maintain the 6.9 kV bus voltage control band given the normal and post-contingency transmission operating voltage band, bounding voltage drop on the grid, and plant conditions. (SSER 22, Section 8.2.2) Closed in SSER 24, Section 8.1. | NRR | Closed |
| (29) | | TVA should provide information about the operating characteristics of the offsite power supply at the Watts Bar Hydro Plant (for dual-unit operation), including the operating voltage range, postcontingency voltage drops (including bounding values and post-unit trip values), and operating frequency range. (SSER 22, Section 8.2.2) (corrected version of Open Item 29 from SSER 22 Appendix HH) Closed in SSER 24, Section 8.1. | NRR | Closed |
| (31) | | TVA should clarify the loading sequence as explained in its letter dated December 6, 2010 to the staff. TVA should clarify whether the existing statements in FSAR regarding automatic sequencing logic are correct. If the FSAR description is correct, TVA should explain how the EDG and logic sequencing circuitry will respond to a LOCA followed by a LOOP scenario. (SSER 22, Section 8.3.1.11) (corrected version of Open Item 31 from SSER 22 Appendix HH) Closed in SSER 24, Section 8.1 | NRR | Closed |

| (34) | CI | TVA stated that the method of compliance with Phase I guidelines would be substantially similar to the current Unit 1 program and that a new Section 3.12 will be added to the Unit 2 FSAR that will be materially equivalent to Section 3.12 of the current Unit 1 FSAR. (SSER 22, Section 9.1.4) Closed in SSER 24, Section 9.1.4. | NRR | Closed |
|---|---|---|---|---|
| (36) | | TVA should provide information to the NRC staff to enable verification that the SGBS meets the requirements and guidance specified in the SER or provide justification that the SGBS meets other standards that demonstrate conformance to GDC 1 and GDC 14. (SSER 22, Section 10.4.8) Closed in SSER 24, Section 10.4.8. | NRR | Closed |
| (44) | | TVA should provide additional information to clarify how the initial and irradiated $RT_{NDT}$ was determined. (SSER 22, Section 5.3.1) Closed in SSER 25, Section 5.3.1. | NRR | Closed |
| (45) | CI | TVA stated in its response to RAI 5.3.2-2, dated July 31, 2010, that the PTLR would be revised to incorporate the COMS arming temperature. (SSER 22, Section 5.3.2) Closed in SSER 25, Section 5.3.2. | NRR | Closed |
| (46) | CI | The LTOP lift settings were not included in the PTLR, but were provided in TVA's response to RAI 5.3.2-2 in its letter dated July 31, 2010. TVA stated in its RAI response that the PTLR would be revised to incorporate the LTOP lift settings into the PTLR. (SSER 22, Section 5.3.2) Closed in SSER 25, Section 5.3.2. | NRR | Closed |
| (62) | CI | Confirm TVA's change to FSAR Section 10.4.9 to reflect its intention to operate with each CST isolated from the other. (SSER 23, Section 10.4.9) Closed in SSER 24, Section 10.4.9. | NRR | Closed |
| (72) | | The NRC staff should complete its review and evaluation of the additional information provided by TVA regarding the ICC instrumentation. (SSER 23, Section 4.4.8) Closed in SSER 25, Section 7.5.2.2. | NRR | Closed |
| (76) | CI | The NRC staff will verify that the derivative time constant is set to zero in WBN Unit 2 before fuel load. (SSER 23, Section 7.8.3) Closed in Inspection Report 05000391/2011607, dated September 30, 2011, ADAMS Accession No. ML112730197. | RII | Closed |
| (78) | | TVA intends to issue a revised calculation reflecting that the TID in the control room is less than $1 \times 10^3$ rads, which will be evaluated by the NRC staff. (SSER 23, Section 7.5.2.3) Closed in SSER 25, Section 7.5.2.3. | NRR | Closed |

| (82) | | The staff concluded that the information provided by TVA pertaining to the in-containment LPMS equipment qualification for vibration was incomplete. TVA should provide (item number 362 of ADAMS Accession No. ML111050009), documentation that demonstrates the LPMS in-containment equipment has been qualified to remain functional in its normal operating vibration environment, per RG 1.133, Revision 1. (SSER 23, Section 7.6.1) Closed in SSER 24, Section 7.6.1.4.5. | NRR | Closed |
| (95) | | TVA should update FSAR Table 7.1-1, "Watts Bar Nuclear Plant NRC Regulatory Guide Conformance," to reference IEEE Std. 603-1991 for the WBN Unit 2 Common Q PAMS. (SSER 23, Section 7.5.2.2.3) Closed in SSER 25, Section 7.5.2.2. | NRR | Closed |
| (96) | | TVA should (1) update FSAR Table 7.1-1 to include RG 1.100, Revision 3, for the Common Q PAMS, or (2) demonstrate that the Common Q PAMS is in conformance with RG 1.100, Revision 1, or provide justification for not conforming. (SSER 23, Section 7.5.2.2.3) Closed in SSER 25, Section 7.5.2.2. | NRR | Closed |
| (97) | | TVA should demonstrate that the WBN Unit 2 Common Q PAMS is in conformance with RG 1.153, Revision 1, or provide justification for not conforming. (SSER 23, Section 7.5.2.2.3) Closed in SSER 25, Section 7.5.2.2. | NRR | Closed |
| (99) | | TVA should update FSAR Table 7.1-1 to reference IEEE 7-4.3.2-2003 as being applicable to the WBN Unit 2 Common Q PAMS. (SSER 23, Section 7.5.2.2.3; SSER 25, Section 7.5.2.2) Closed in SSER 25, Section 7.5.2.2. | NRR | Closed |
| (100) | | TVA should update FSAR Table 7.1-1 to reference RG 1.168, Revision 1; IEEE 1012-1998; and IEEE 1028-1997 as being applicable to the WBN Unit 2 Common Q PAMS. (SSER 23, Section 7.5.2.2.3) Closed in SSER 25, Section 7.5.2.2. | NRR | Closed |
| (102) | | TVA should update FSAR Table 7.1-1 to reference RG 1.209 and IEEE Std. 323-2003 as being applicable to the WBN Unit 2 Common Q PAMS. (SSER 23, Section 7.5.2.2.3) Closed in SSER 25, Section 7.5.2.2. | NRR | Closed |
| (103) | | TVA should demonstrate that the WBN Unit 2 Common Q PAMS conforms to RG 1.209 and IEEE Std. 323-2003, or provide justification for not conforming. (SSER 23, Section 7.5.2.2.3) Closed in SSER 25, Section 7.5.2.2. | NRR | Closed |
| (104) | CI | The NRC staff will review the WEC self assessment to verify that it the WBN Unit 2 PAMS is compliant to the V&V requirements in the SPM or that deviations | NRR | Closed |

| | | | | |
|---|---|---|---|---|
| | | from the requirements are adequately justified. (SSER 23, Section 7.5.2.2.3.4.2) Closed in SSER 25, Section 7.5.2.2. | | |
| (106) | | TVA should produce a final WBN Unit 2 Common Q PAMS SRS that is independently reviewed. (SSER 23, Section 7.5.2.2.3.4.3.1) Closed in SSER 25, Section 7.5.2.2. | NRR | Closed |
| (107) | CI | TVA should provide to the NRC staff documentation to confirm that the final WBN Unit 2 Common Q PAMS SDDs that are independently reviewed. (SSER 23, Section 7.5.2.2.3.4.3.2) Closed in SSER 25, Section 7.5.2.2. | NRR | Closed |
| (109) | | TVA should demonstrate to the NRC staff acceptable data storm testing of the Common Q PAMS. (SSER 23, Section 7.5.2.2.3.7.1.8) Closed in SSER 25, Section 7.5.2.2. | NRR | Closed |
| (119) | | TVA should submit WNA-CN-00157-WBT, Revision 0, to the NRC by letter. The NRC staff should confirm by review of WNA-CN-00157-WBT, Revision 0, that no credible source of faulting can negatively impact the CETs or PAMS train. (SSER 24, Section 7.7.1.9.5) Closed in SSER 25, Section 7.7.1.9. | NRR | Closed |
| (122) | | TVA should confirm to the NRC staff that different divisions of safety power are supplied to the IIS SPS cabinets, with the power cables routed in separate shielded conduits. (SSER 24, Section 7.7.1.9.5) Closed in SSER 25, Section 7.7.1.9. | NRR | Closed |
| (124) | | While the BEACON datalink on the Application server can connect to either BEACON machine, only BEACON A is used for communication. TVA should clarify to the NRC staff whether automatic switchover to the other server is not permitted. (SSER 24, Section 7.7.1.9.5) Closed in SSER 25, Section 7.7.1.9. | NRR | Closed |
| (128) | | TVA should submit the seismic qualification test report procedures and results for the SPS cabinets to the NRC staff for review. (SSER 24, Section 7.7.1.9.5) Closed in SSER 25, Section 7.7.1.9. | NRR | Closed |
| (130) | | TVA should provide a summary to the NRC staff of the EMC qualification test results of the SPS cabinets. (SSER 24, Section 7.7.1.9.5) Closed in SSER 25, Section 7.7.1.9. | NRR | Closed |
| (135) | | TVA has not provided the analysis required by 10 CFR Part 50, Appendix I, subsection II.D. TVA must demonstrate with a cost-benefit analysis that a sufficient reduction in the collective dose to the public within a 50-mile radius would not be achieved by reasonable changes to the design of the WBN gaseous effluent processing systems. (SSER 24, | NRR | Closed |

| | | Section 11.3) Closed in SSER 25, Section 11.3. | | |
|---|---|---|---|---|

CI – Confirmatory Issue

| NRC FORM 335<br>(12-2010)<br>NRCMD 3.7 | U.S. NUCLEAR REGULATORY COMMISSION | 1. REPORT NUMBER<br>(Assigned by NRC, Add Vol., Supp., Rev.,<br>and Addendum Numbers, if any.) |
|---|---|---|
| **BIBLIOGRAPHIC DATA SHEET**<br>*(See instructions on the reverse)* | | NUREG-0847<br>Supplement No. 25 |

| 2. TITLE AND SUBTITLE | 3. DATE REPORT PUBLISHED | |
|---|---|---|
| Safety Evaluation Report<br>Related to the Operation of<br>Watts Bar Nuclear Plant Unit 2<br>Docket No. 50-391 | MONTH | YEAR |
| | December | 2011 |
| | 4. FIN OR GRANT NUMBER | |

| 5. AUTHOR(S) | 6. TYPE OF REPORT |
|---|---|
| J. Poole, et al. | Technical |
| | 7. PERIOD COVERED *(Inclusive Dates)* |

8. PERFORMING ORGANIZATION - NAME AND ADDRESS *(If NRC, provide Division, Office or Region, U.S. Nuclear Regulatory Commission, and mailing address; if contractor, provide name and mailing address.)*

U.S. Nuclear Regulatory Commission
Office of Nuclear Reactor Regulation
Division of Operating Reactor Licensing
Washington, DC 20555-0001

9. SPONSORING ORGANIZATION - NAME AND ADDRESS *(If NRC, type "Same as above"; if contractor, provide NRC Division, Office or Region, U.S. Nuclear Regulatory Commission, and mailing address.)*

Same as above.

10. SUPPLEMENTARY NOTES
Docket No. 50-391

11. ABSTRACT *(200 words or less)*

This report supplements the safety evaluation report (SER), NUREG-0847 (June 1982), Supplement No. 24 (September 2011; Agencywide Documents Access and Management System (ADAMS) Accession No. ML11277A148), with respect to the application filed by the Tennessee Valley Authority (TVA), as applicant and owner, for a license to operate Watts Bar Nuclear Plant (WBN) Unit 2 (Docket No. 50-391).

In its SER and supplemental SER (SSER) Nos. 1 through 20 issued by the U.S Nuclear Regulatory Commission (NRC) staff, the NRC staff documented its safety evaluation and determination that WBN Unit 1 met all applicable regulatory requirements. Based on its evaluation and satisfactory inspection findings, the NRC issued a full-power operating license for WBN Unit 1 on February 7, 1996.

In SSERs subsequent to SSER 20, the staff addressed TVA's application for a license to operate WBN Unit 2, and provided information regarding the status of items remaining to be resolved, which were open at the time that TVA deferred construction of WBN Unit 2, and which were not evaluated and resolved as part of licensing for WBN Unit 1. In this and future SSERs, the staff will document its evelution and closure of open items in its review of TVA's application for an operating license for WBN Unit 2.

| 12. KEY WORDS/DESCRIPTORS *(List words or phrases that will assist researchers in locating the report.)* | 13. AVAILABILITY STATEMENT |
|---|---|
| Safety Evaluation Report (SER)<br>Watts Bar Nuclear Plant<br>Docket No. 50-391 | unlimited |
| | 14. SECURITY CLASSIFICATION |
| | *(This Page)*<br>unclassified |
| | *(This Report)*<br>unclassified |
| | 15. NUMBER OF PAGES |
| | 16. PRICE |

NRC FORM 335 (12-2010)

December 2011

Safety Evaluation Report Related to the Operation of
Watts Bar Nuclear Plant, Unit 2

NUREG-0847
Supplement 25

UNITED STATES
NUCLEAR REGULATORY COMMISSION
WASHINGTON, DC 20555-0001

OFFICIAL BUSINESS